SEEING

IN INTIMACY AND PSYCHOTHERAPY

J.D. GILL, PH.D.

Create Space
2016

BOOKS BY J.D. GILL

FORMS OF LIFE and other essays
LETTERS TO JIM
FINDING HUMAN
LETTERS OF JULIET to the Knight in Rusty Armor
  Second Edition
ONE HUNDRED REASONS WHY I LOVE YOU
CIRCUMFERENCE a memoir
THE MISERY OF THE GOOD CHILD
IN-BETWEEN selected poems from 1962 - 1996
RECURRING THEMES IN THE TAROT AND THE
SELF
MEXICO PAPERS VOLS 1 - 3

Vision is the art of seeing what is invisible to others.

—Jonathan Swift

CONTENTS

FORWARD

It is widely known we vary in how tall or short we are. There are differences in our weight, financial status, and IQ. But it is less widely accepted there are differences in our ability to see.

Just plain see.

Some people are able to see an amazing amount of what is around them. Others are only able to see little.

Being unable to see in any significant sense is akin to the lack of a musical ear.

If no one can see you (find you), you will lose yourself. It is only if you can be seen that you will be able to know who you are. Millions of people are never seen. Never found.

We are profoundly interpersonal creatures, and as a result we only function optimally in relationship with others— either in person or in our minds.

Our ability to see depends on multiple factors, not the least of which is our ability to grasp subtlety and nuance. That is, some of us make general distinctions. Others are able to see in much finer detail.

Part of this is a function of education. The more we learn about, for example, psychology or steam engines, the finer will be the distinctions we are able to make about those things. This holds for most other topics as well.

Another way in which we differ is our ability to use the grammar of the language and especially our use of the device called metaphor. In a linguistic sense it is metaphor that allows us to extend our gaze beyond the surface.

The ability to see beyond the surface plays an important role in intimacy and also in psychotherapy. If for no other reason, intimacy and psychotherapy require significantly more than a superficial view.

In *The Little Prince,* Saint-Exupery wrote:

> Here is my secret. It is very simple. One
> only sees well with the heart. What is essen-
> tial is invisible to the eyes.

Both intimacy and psychotherapy involve us as people in our deepest sense. Becoming better at genuinely seeing people and also better at functioning in intimate interactions will—all things being equal—go a long way toward making our lives richer, and far more fulfilling.

CHAPTER ONE: FIRST MEETING

When you first meet another person what do you know about him or her?

The answer is: very little.

You can see how he or she is dressed. You can try to gauge if he or she is friendly or not. You can learn the person's name. You can feel intrigued by him or her or not. You can feel repelled.

You might strike up a conversation and listen to what he or she chooses to talk about. You may ask him or her questions. He or she may ask you questions.

Whether your meeting is casual or an instance of psychotherapy many of the same principles apply. That is: in order to establish any sort of intimacy or to do psychotherapy you must be able to (at least begin to) develop a working interpersonal connection.

How to do that?

We as people exist in contexts. *When you first meet a person or a patient you have before you the outcome or result of a life lived in the context from which the person has come.* Just as language operates within a context, so do people. And just as an important part of understanding language consists of being aware of the context in which it is used, so with people, it is important to be aware of the contexts they inhabit as well as the contexts in which they grew.

This is to say human behavior is a product of contexts. It simply cannot exist outside of them—even if such a thing could be imagined.

Teenagers use the word "sick" as a synonym of "terrific." My generation referred to the "best" as "cool." These are idiomatic instances, but, clearly, in these cases one has to grasp the context to grasp how the words are being used.

Tuning into the relevant context is closely related to genuinely listening and seeing. Obviously if you see the context in which someone operates, you see more than one does whose seeing doesn't extend that far. The more one sees, the more one is therefore able to understand.

Each of us grew in different families, comprised of different people, who lived in different places. There can be dramatic differences within each town as well as dramatic differences within each family. No two persons have the "same" experience, though it may be similar.

A patient will likely say what brought him or her to consult the therapist. Called the "presenting problem," this issue will be a function of the context of the patient. I am stressing this point on purpose. *It is as important to learn about the context as it is to learn about the complaint.*

In a somewhat like fashion there is a concept in art that concerns the difference between positive and negative spaces. Here, space that is not taken up by the figure must be as interesting as space taken up by the figure. In this way the entire work is interesting.

In similar fashion a therapist must pay attention to what is not said as well as to what is said.

The concern for the context is what led Freud to focus on early development. One's personality pattern has been importantly formed by the experiences one has had. In fact, it may be said a distorted personality is the result of a distorted context.

The distorted context is the result of two people (parents) who themselves came from distorted contexts of their own. The distorted contexts go on "unto the seventh generation" if not longer.

This is not a license to blame one's parents for all one's troubles, but it *is* to point out the troubles began there. That is where one got the dent, but the dent is now something one has, not one's parents. Therefore, it is up to the person him or herself to deal with the dent he or she has sustained. Blaming does not solve anything.

The point is that in getting to know another you need to learn more about him or her. You might want to learn about his or her childhood. Where was this person born? What kind of work did his or her father do? His or her mother? What was the father like? The mother? Did the person have brothers and/or sisters? Who was oldest? What were the brothers and/or sisters like? What are they doing now?

These kinds of questions begin to allow for a sense of the childhood context of the other. Answers begin to give you a feel for the person

It is, however, important to hold the answers you get as hypotheses instead of truths. People, ourselves included, don't always give straight information. A terrible father may be reported to be "good" for example.

To really get to know another, you might learn about what things he or she likes and admires. What attitudes and biases does he or she have? To what things is this person drawn? Art? Sports? Music? What kinds of art, sports, or music? Why?

What are the person's hopes and dreams? What is most important to him or her? What is his or her deepest regret?

The more completely you can fill in the details of the formative background context, the more completely you can be able to understand the person.

Omitting this information condemns you to operate on the surface with another. Intimacy of any sort will not be possible, and psychotherapy will consist only of topological or surface issues. In an important sense you will miss the richness of the person involved.

In this sense psychotherapy is a special kind of intimacy.

It is a kind of intimacy without any acting on romantic and/ or sexual feelings if any. This is important.

It is only within the safety generated by a genuine openness without the contaminating involvement of romantic and/or sexual behavior that psychotherapy is able to do what it needs to do.

Thus feelings may be thought of as one thing. Acting on those feelings is quite something else. There are many things that may be done with a feeling. It may be acted on, avoided, channeled into something else, worked out in elaborate fantasies, &c.

One of the most valuable things that can be done with a feeling is to *talk about it*. That is, talk about it without acting on it. This, it turns out, is a safe way to manage feelings, and it is the essence of both intimacy and psychotherapy.

It is also important to remember that stress routinely affects the ways in which we behave and communicate. Meeting someone for the first time is not the same thing as meeting them for the hundredth time. People who enter psychotherapy are *always* under stress. Not only are they meeting an unknown person (the therapist), but they are wondering whether or not they will be able to trust that person.

Lovers can spend all day getting ready for a date. Really. They do this so they will appear natural to another? Hardly. It is entirely possible both people are trying to appear at their best for each other. That leaves most of who the persons actually are out of sight.

The point is not trivial. In order to see another, you may have to be able to experience him or her in more than one situation in order to get any sort of clear picture.

The first meeting with another is an instance of interaction with that person, but it is only that. Nonetheless, it is a very important interaction. If nothing else, it typically reveals what the person felt he or she would convey in the meeting. That is to say the person made some sort of impression. This information helps in learning who he or she is.

Of course first impressions are not always very adequate, but they *are* important in that they are a sample of how this other person is routinely seen. When later impressions counter these the disparity may be noticed.

CHAPTER TWO: A LITERARY EXAMPLE

A literary example illustrates the points I have been making. This example begins with the first paragraph of Flannery O'Connor's novel *Wise Blood*. It is a bit overdone for our purposes, but it is a good example as it involves a first meeting between readers and the characters in the story.

Here is the first paragraph:

> Hazel Motes sat at a forward angle on the green plush train seat, looking one minute at the window as if he might want to jump out of it, and the next down the aisle at the other end of the car. The train was racing through tree tops that fell away at intervals and showed the sun standing, very red, on the edge of the farthest woods. Nearer, the plowed fields curved and faded and the few hogs nosing in the furrows looked like large spotted stones. Mrs. Wally Bee Hitchcock, who was facing Motes in the section, said that she thought the early evening like this was the prettiest time of day and she asked him if he didn't think so too. She was a fat woman with pink collars and cuffs and pear-shaped legs that slanted off the train seat and didn't reach the floor (O'Connor, 1962, p. 1).

What do we learn from this paragraph? First and foremost, Hazel is sitting at a forward angle. Is this a comfortable position? No. It suggests what? He is tense and on edge?

What about Mrs. Hitchcock? Does it matter that she doesn't have her own name? Of course. She tries to make small talk with an odd-appearing, total stranger. What does this suggest? She is narrow and likely has no real experience beyond her small circle? There one makes small talk? She simply assumes this situation will be like the ones she already knows and forges ahead?

She is fat and wears pink collars and cuffs. What does this manner of dress tell us? Does she seem intelligent?

The interaction continues:

> He looked at her a second and, without answering, leaned forward and stared down the length of the car again...
>
> "I guess you're going home," she said, turning back to him again. He didn't look, to her, much over twenty, but he had a stiff black broad-brimmed hat on his lap, a hat that an elderly country preacher would wear. His suit was a glaring blue and the price tag was still stapled on the sleeve of it.

This is more information. Mrs. Hitchcock keeps at it. She doesn't seem adept at picking up subtle (and not so subtle) cues. How about Hazel? He looks young, and he has a flat hat like a country preacher would wear. Is that important? What does it suggest? Does it matter that Hazel has not uttered a word?

More information:

> He didn't answer her or move his eyes from whatever he was looking at. The sack at his feet was an army duffel bag and she decided that he had been in the army and had been released and that now he was going home. She wanted to get close enough to see what the suit had cost him but she found herself squinting instead at his eyes, trying almost to look into them. They were the color of pecan shells and set in deep sockets. The outline of a skull under his skin was plain and insistent.

The picture begins to clarify. Hazel is a young man just from the army. What does it mean he didn't bother to remove the tag from his suit? Would you do that? Does it suggest unconcern? Impatience? Ignorance? Or is Hazel just crazy?

His eyes are deep set suggesting what? He is haunted? He is driven? He is scary?

She felt irked and wrenched her attention loose and squinted at the price tag. The suit had cost him $11.98. She felt that placed him and looked at his face again as if she were fortified against it now...his eyes were what held her attention longest. Their settings were so deep that they seemed, to her, almost like passages leading somewhere and she leaned halfway across the space that separated the two seats, trying to see into them. He turned toward the window suddenly...

"Well," Mrs. Hitchcock said, "there's no place like home."

Here we learn that Mrs. Hitchcock is not only unintelligent but also shallow. She rates people the way she rates the prices of things. The two, we imagine, are the same to her. But Hazel has bewitching eyes. There is something complex going on behind them, something likely out of reach of the capacities of Mrs. Hitchcock.

From this example it is possible to illustrate the kinds of cues it is important to pick up in order to learn about someone one has not met before. Each small piece of information is helpful in developing an impression.

Clothes may or may not matter. Manner of speaking almost always does. Is the person articulate? Does the person have easy eye contact (without paying attention to it)?

How about grammatical usage? Grooming? Does this person make an emotional impact?

Most significant of all, does the person appear to have a functioning empathic sense?   Is there empathic resonance—a mutual emotional experience? Is the person likable? Not likable?   Why? Is it easy to talk to this person or is it not?

It is by asking questions like this, you will be able to form hypotheses. These hypotheses, hopefully, will be refined again and again over the course of the meeting. It is how a sense of understanding begins. The important point here is it depends on *seeing*.   The more that is seen the better the resulting hypotheses will be.

In addition to how someone appears, it is important to notice what it is he or she talks about. It is appropriate to constantly wonder why talk about that?   Why talk about that now? Why talk about that like that? What could this mean?

Related to this is the theme. What keeps reappearing? Does it reappear obviously or by innuendo? Does it make sense?

It is best to allow the stranger or the patient to make his or her own impression with as little interference as possible. This will be his or her idea of what would matter to you. Remember, if this is a patient, this person came in for help. What kind of help do they have in mind?

An initial meeting with someone will result in one's having an impression of the other. This is an important beginning point if for no other reason than it is how the person likely affects everybody else. The person may not be aware of the impact he or she has and may, therefore, be puzzled by the responses he or she receives in return.

The initial meeting will also result in one's having a feeling about the person. This is similarly important for like reasons. It is always important to ask oneself, how does this person make me feel? If one is reasonably open and provides an environment in which the other feels 1) safe and 2) welcome, the feeling one has may be of critical importance.

The optimal attitude for one to have when meeting a stranger is a neutral one that conveys a willingness to hear along with a lack of judgment. Nothing shuts off disclosure like a judgmental context.

The initial neutral context is important as it allows for the thoughts and feelings of the two people involved to occur in the least biased way.

Nonetheless it may be said the interviewer always has an advantage that the person interviewed does not have: the interviewer sees the person from the *outside*. The person is seen as other. This is important as an inside view and an outside view are rarely, if ever, the same.

It may be very early to notice mismatches between inside and outside views, but they are important. The most cutting and judgmental person I knew in college told me one night, "I may have my flaws, but I am an essentially loving person." I almost swallowed my tongue.

It is also early to scan for flexibility, but one may notice tendencies in either on overly-rigid or an overly-vague pattern.

All these hypotheses can be followed up as meetings progress.

— —-

The passages by Flannery O'Connor may be illuminated further.

Sparrow (see Sparrow) said:

> ...I mentioned the importance of vision for the serious novelist and by vision I didn't just mean the faculty of sight. I meant the gift of being able to see into things, which is the religious dimension of vision and this is the thread that runs through all of Flannery O'- Connor's work.

Indeed, O'Connor herself remarked:

> The Southern writer is forced from all sides to make his gaze extend beyond the surface,

beyond mere problems, until it touches that realm which is the concern of prophets and poets (O'Connor, 1960).

One might add: "and psychologists and lovers." This will be the case if by psychologists one is describing those who are always searching for more information about another, a different point of view, a better insight. Of course in any ultimate sense, another cannot ever be fully known—whatever that might be, but it is hard to see how more information will not be helpful.

Science, on the other hand, tends to be a formal operation that seeks understanding on the basis of empirical factors. That is its area.

It is easy, however, to see that empirical factors do not comprise the entirety of *human* experience. Feelings, for example, are frequently omitted in empirical pursuits. This is O'Connor's point.

O'Connor (Ibid) said:

> Since the eighteenth century, the popular spirit of each succeeding age has tended more and more to the view that the ills and mysteries of life will eventually fall before the scientific advances of man...[here] actions are predetermined by psychic make-up or the economic situation or some other determinable factor, then he [the investigator] will be concerned above all with an accurate reproduction of the things that most immediately concern man, with the

natural forces that he feels control his destiny.

The notion that science will be able to answer all questions is called "scientism" in scientific circles. Properly speaking it is not a part of science

Nonetheless, it is important not to "throw the baby out with the bath water" and conclude that since science does not have *everything* to offer, it therefore has no*thing* to offer. It only has science to offer.

There are, for example, developed systems of psychotherapy and human interaction that have been developed within the area of science. Clearly these are important findings.

In this regard, there are categories of personality patterns that have been developed and are extremely useful in clinical applications for understanding personality types. Neuropsychology has important insights to offer.

The scientifically and clinically derived classification system is in fact necessary for any very thorough seeing and understanding of another person. This is true simply because the sheer amount of information that applies to a person quickly becomes overwhelming. Having a system of categories or slots into which to sort the information in manageable amounts is enormously helpful. Insights gained over years and years of clinical practice with a wide range of people may be used to augment present information and allow for more effective interactions.

These categories or slots need to be "held lightly," however. As Aristotle (see Aristotle) pointed out, classification systems are not reality in themselves. They are, rather, ways to organize reality.

Seeing is essential. No amount of test data, classification schema, or theoretical constructs allow for a *close view*. It is important to additionally consider an individual person in his or her individual context to get a picture clear enough for intimacy and/or psychotherapy.

The issue here is that classification categories are essentially developed to fit groups of people who may or may not be similar in subtle ways. Though the categories may be a good place to start, it is *always* important to move beyond the categories to affect an understanding of an individual person.

O'Connor (Ibid) said:

> On the other hand, if the writer believes that our life is and will remain essentially mysterious, if he looks upon us as beings existing in a created order to whose laws we freely respond, then what he sees on the surface will be of interest to him only as he can go through it into an experience of mystery itself...the meaning of a story [or understanding] does not begin except at a depth where adequate motivation and adequate psychology and the various determinations have been exhausted. Such a writer will be interested in what we don't understand rather than in what we do.

This is to stress the need for abilities *beyond* those of science, not necessarily those *instead* of science. Still, at the same time, the area beyond science is important.

Die-hard apologists of the scientific approach are actually identifying themselves as rigid in their thinking and are unable to pursue alternate avenues for personal reasons. Again, good therapists are identified by what they are willing to *not* know as much as they are identified by what they know.

This extends to all manner of test information as well as the evidence of experimental practices. Becoming an adequate therapist requires study into what has traditionally been called "human."

In fact, science may not be the first place to turn in order to learn about what it is to be human. The existence of mythology, religion, and poetry may be a better source.

This is the case as over the history of human existence we have developed two different kinds of speech. One type *describes* and another type *evokes*.

Metaphor is the device that evokes. It allows us to talk about feelings and experiences beyond the capacity of simple expression.

My favorite example is from *Macbeth* (See Shakespeare):

...sleep that knits up the raveled sleeve of care.

This image has an emotional resonance in addition to describing the fact that things often look different after a good night's sleep. One is less stressed, more rested.

Saying "I love you with all my heart" is a metaphor. "I hate your guts" is another. "I am coming apart" and "I feel like hell" are others.

If we had not developed metaphor, all we would have would be history—a collection of facts and figures. The emotional dimension of human existence—how people felt and what they cared about—would have been left out.

A great many, if not most, of the ways we describe psychological dimensions are by using metaphors. They allow us to talk about these things in an understandable and immediate way.

CHAPTER THREE: SOMETIMES SEEING IS A FEELING

We had an expression at the hospital where I practiced. If, say, someone had made us worry, feel bad, feel inadequate, or feel miserable—we said the other had "put the stink on us."

"The stink" was a feeling we did not have before our interaction with this other person, and it was a feeling we could avoid by not interacting with that person. Clearly "the stink" was a result of our interaction we had with that other person.

This, we realized, is tremendously important information. It is likely what happened is that the other person put his or her feeling *into* us. Now we had the feeling too.

In psychoanalysis this is called *projective identification* and it is an essential element of how people can communicate.

In projective identification one projects (puts) one's feelings *into* the other, not *onto* the other. Thus the other has the feeling now and feels—since he or she is feeling it—it must be theirs. But it is not.

It is important to ask oneself, *"Whose feeling is it I am having now?"* It may be mine, but it might belong to someone else. If one gets this feeling routinely when one interacts with a person, and one does not get this feeling when interacting with others, it may safely be thought the feeling belongs not to oneself but to the other.

Actually, this is one way in which one can learn the most about another person. Instead of telling you about his or her feeling, he or she simply gives it to you so you can feel it too. Often this is done unconsciously by the other person who feels he or she is successfully hiding or disguising the feeling from your view.

For example, I may feel unusually bored in the presence of another person. I check myself and find I don't routinely feel this way in the presence of others. What could this mean?

It is possible the other person is afraid of me or frightened of others in general and is adding as much distance as he or she can to the interaction. I feel I am sitting there alone. I may begin to fall asleep. I may ask, "Why does this person need so much distance between us?".

I may find I feel hopelessly inadequate and stupid around a person, and I don't feel this way around others.

On the other hand, I may feel unusually important and knowledgeable around a person and not around others.

The list goes on and on.

A patient once asked me in a perturbed tone, "Have you ever helped anybody?" The message was: "you idiot." Also in this situation, I *felt* like an idiot as well—so the communication was successful.

However, it was important in that situation to question whether or not the patient might be the one who was feeling stupid. I decided to go with that interpretation until shown to be otherwise and thus was able to be compassionate instead of angry. Compassion moved the interaction in a different direction from the one anger would have done.

This is one way arguments and fights can happen. It is also how love happens.

In both intimacy and psychotherapy, it is important to remember that there are many ways to deal with a feeling. In this instance I am describing, it is important to *catch* the feeling so I don't simply act on it as if it were my own. If I can catch it and then talk about it, understanding may be the result.

However, it is also important to point out that the person projecting (putting out) the feeling may not know he or she is doing so. If you accuse him or her of projecting the feeling, you are most likely going to receive a *denial*.

Are you "nuts?"

The best way to deal with a feeling you have caught and feel has come from another is to keep it in mind as an hypothesis to be used in constructing an understanding of the other.

It is also possible to *join with* another person in a feeling. This might happen when the other has had a profound experience and begins to tear up. You may find yourself beginning to tear up as well.

In this instance it may be said you have moved close to the other person such that you are *resonating* with the feeling he or she is having.

Resonating with another person's feelings is the basis of intimacy and also significant psychotherapy as it shows the two of you are profoundly together in the experience.

This extreme sort of togetherness is entirely different from, say, passing strangers on Fifth Avenue. It may be said to be relating with the *whole person* rather than the surface.

When it comes to understanding, seeing and feeling are interwoven. Seeing beyond the surface has an emotional component, and this is important as the emotional component may *agree* with the seeing component or it may *disagree*.

When there is disagreement between these factors the situation may be said to be *paradoxical*. That is, so to speak, one message is being transmitted on one channel, and another message is being transmitted on another channel *at the same time*.

The resulting feeling may be that of being handed a dead fish. The other person seems to be pleased but not really. Success has never felt so flat or so awful. The other seems to be saying "yes" but it feels like "no."

For example, two colleagues may have agreed to go to a film together. The time, date, and place have been set. Two hours before the film begins, one person learns of a lecture she really wants to attend. She calls the other person and tells her the situation—saying she can't make the film.

"I'm sorry to do this; I hope you will understand," she says.

"Its no problem," says the other. She says this, however, with the tone of "You are the worst slime in the universe."

The friendship becomes strained. The first person thought it was okay she attended the lecture. The second person, however, said it was okay on the *content* level, but her method of saying it on the *feeling* level was just the opposite.

This is how information can be conveyed without having to take responsibility for it. Only the seeing (or overt) part needs to be owned. The other (the covert part, the feeling) can be denied entirely.

Such interactions may be crazy making.

The important question here is why does this other person need to remain so hidden? Why does he or she have to deny how he or she is feeling?

Learning to read the feeling level of interactions provides a richness that reading only the seeing level lacks. The two levels together may be thought to constitute a complete communication. And since one level may be admitted and another denied, a situation may be established in which a tremendous amount of information can be passed to another without a word being said.

It is this situation that can occur when one "falls out of love." It is possible to continue the surface behavior, but the underlying feeling has shifted. This is also what can happen in psychotherapy when the therapist has unwittingly been caught up in the patient's world—thus erasing the distance necessary for adequate therapeutic perception.

Also, any time the therapist gets caught up in his or her own world, focus on the patient is minimized. It is important to ask oneself why does this seem to be happening? Why here?

Camus (1956) remarked that modern Christianity is a giant laundry venture that has run out of soap. Thus everything tumbles around, but nothing gets clean. That is, the message is present on the surface, but the depth message has been lost.

Being unguarded is to be open with one's thoughts and feelings as one is able to grasp them. This will allow another to know the most possible about one's own view of oneself. Conversely not allowing access to one's thoughts and feelings will keep others at maximum distance.

A feeling may be used as a "set up." That is to say the feeling of another may be used as a manipulation in order to compel one to respond in a certain fashion.

When teaching psychotherapy students my brother John used to say, "Trust your instincts and do the opposite." This, he thought, was the essence of psychotherapy.

He was responding to the fact that we often unconsciously try to "pull" a favorable response from another. For example, I may come across in a meek and needy way. This routinely gets a helping response from others. Thus, it may be said I "pull" helping responses from others. It is the way I interact.

Families and close relationships may exist in a blizzard of both over the table and under the table interactions. These may be either acknowledged or denied, but they have enormous power in shaping the ongoing patterns of the family or group.

There may be an unwritten rule that mother is in charge, an unwritten rule that the second child is the problem, &c. Patients bring these unwritten rules with them when they enter psychotherapy. Aspects of their behavior may not be sensible until the rule and how it operates is uncovered.

When you encounter this kind of pattern on the part of another, you are able to learn important information about the context in which he or she has been living. This is true as the action you observe likely works in his or her natural context. That, further, may be why it has never been called to his or her attention. To him or her it is simply part of the air.

CHAPTER FOUR: SOMETIMES SEEING IS A RE-QUIREMENT

There are situations in which some kinds of interactions are allowed and others are not. That is, the *range* of interactions is restricted in some way.

Some people behave as if there is a line that must not be crossed. There may be topics that are outlawed.

In this situation what is included and what is excluded comprises important information.

People have all sorts of biases and prejudices. Knowing this is important in knowing the people themselves.

For example, it may not be possible to talk about books with someone. It just doesn't interest him or her. It may not be possible to talk about sports.

More subtly it may not be possible to talk about sadness. Happy times or travel may be off the list. It may not be possible to talk about one's children, about food, or about the films one admires.

The things that can be talked about as well as the things that cannot be talked about constitute important information about a person. There is always a *reason* these things are the case. The reasons may or may not be able to be discussed.

Sometimes topics are simply avoided. Sometimes they are pointedly outlawed. Again, there is a reason for these patterns.

When the restriction is not related to specific topics or areas, it may be of a different form. For example, a person may subtly avoid any mention of any kind of emotional depth related to anything.

It is said we can only know what we know. It is very difficult to know what we don't know.

There are many ways to deal with this situation. One might struggle to learn more about what one doesn't know. One may read, discuss as widely as one can with as many people as one can. One may seek as many different experiences as one is able to have, as each experience provides a different point of view. One may enter psychotherapy to find out what one doesn't know, &c.

Conversely, one may try to block out everything one doesn't know. One may restrict his or her input to a single or a few sources and avoid all others. Where I came from this was called being a "one trick pony." Thus I might be highly adept at knowing one sort of thing but astonishingly unaware of others.

I may pretend to learn new things. I may pretend to avoid new things. There are many options.

The important point concerns my attitude about new things. There are people who rush toward them, and there are people who avoid them at all cost.

Related to this are people who have never moved beyond one essential context. Everything is interpreted in terms of this context. It seems such people have never experienced another point of perspective—and if they have, they rejected it. To them there is only one experiential base possible. It may be felt all others are "wrong."

I had a patient for whom this was a rather elaborate defense. He was an adult professor, and yet he was curiously attached to his home town experience. Whatever he heard, he altered so it would fit into his home town experience. If one tried to give him some new bit of information, he would respond to this by ignoring it and giving a bit of his own information.

It was as if he had stopped growing at some point and had decided to see the whole world as supporting his original point of view.

This was how this person kept himself from growing and learning new things. Whatever was new was reshaped by him to fit in with what was already known.

As a result of a long and difficult exploration it became clear this person had a deep-seated feeling of inadequacy. But, rather than work to become more adequate, he—at some point simply decided to proclaim himself adequate at the level he had then achieved. Thus his feelings of inadequacy were solved.

Yet, it order to maintain the feeling he was adequate, he had to transform all input into something he already knew. This is how he was able to maintain his sense of esteem.

It was also the way he avoided doing any serious work in psychotherapy. Adept at his pattern, he was able to be triumphant.

The problem was that he was depressed. This he denied as well. Yet it was difficult to be around him and his depression as this was highly contagious. It was amazingly difficult to simply sit with him for an hour.

Despite being very bright, this person was unable to tell me any of this. And, to be fair, I was unable to tell him about it without activating his pattern. It was air tight.

I resolved to listen to him compassionately as someone who could do nothing else. That I was kind with him and highly involved slowly allowed him to soften a bit and to trust information with me.

It was *very* slow going as each step he took was a risk to his esteem. I was well aware that any empathic failure on my part would cause his defenses to close, and all progress to stop.

An additional example of this defense appears in the beginning essay of *Forms of Life and Other Essays* (Gill, 2014).

Another way in which a requirement may be seen is the case of someone who appears normal but who has limited capacity.

Here one may have acquired fairly adequate social and life skills, but he or she can only go so far. It is a bit of the case of the car that just can't go any faster. It looks as if it could go faster, but it can't.

Thus one is always expecting the other person to have abilities he or she simply doesn't have.

The person also cannot tell you this, as they either 1) don't know it or 2) assume you already know it.

The result is a constant mismatch that may quickly become frustrating for both parties concerned.

It is polite to adapt oneself to the capacity of another and maximize whatever interaction is possible within that dimension.

Attempting to push a person beyond his or her ability will result in chaos all around.

Such restrictions may be characteristic of the entire context in which a person was raised and lives. The whole group of family and friends may be compromised in terms of education, employment options, cultural level, pursuits, &c.

This is being mentioned as such a situation is typically discovered slowly in the course of the interaction. Initially, the interaction context may not seem limited. Only with increasing interaction does the limitation appear.

For certain groups of people, the limitation is the source of their difficulties in living. One such group is known in psychological circles as Borderline Personality Disorder.

In this instance people tend to see the world in black and white terms. Something is either good or it is bad. If it isn't good, it is bad. Obviously. There is no in between.

Such a structure makes it extremely difficult for a person to learn new things or correct something about him or herself The reason for this is that it is thought to be bad if one doesn't know something (already), and it is bad if there is something about oneself that could be improved.

This kind of person needs the other person to be at fault in any kind of conflict for the same reason. The logic is I can't be at fault, because that is bad. I, of course, can't be the bad one, so it must be your fault. This is how I maintain my very fragile sense of esteem.

It is easy to see why such people have a tough time in the world. By ten AM each day, the world has managed to prove itself to be a bad place.

Even worse, lovers and therapists are also bad people. They get most everything wrong, and it is all their fault. Further, they are disgustingly difficult to shape up.

One would think it would be natural to avoid other people since they are so bad. But I can't leave them, because then I have nobody. Thus I hate them, but I don't want them to leave me. Ever.

The result is a fraught interaction that is usually highly emotionally volatile. Strong feelings are involved and shift frequently. There may be no way to keep the focus on progress as the issue of who is right and who is wrong takes precedence.

All people have limits. None of us know everything and can do everything. It is, however, one thing to know one's limits and abilities and be willing to acknowledge them and quite another thing to deny their existence and force other people to act as if these limits and restricted abilities simply don't exist.

If the restriction is not due to a limit of capacity, it is likely due to an emotional pattern that was learned and practiced in one's past context—or a limitation that pertains to the present interaction.

In any case it is important to *notice* the restriction and attempt to *decode* it so that a more adequate view of the situation may be found.

CHAPTER FIVE: SOMETIMES SEEING IS GRASPING THE CONTEXT

Consider, for example, a person who has been raised in a home in which the parents were avid outdoors people. There was nothing more important to them than camping and fishing. The parents had little use for school beyond high school and both of them were very devoted to their jobs. The father worked in a warehouse, and the mother was a file clerk at a corporate office.

The child was provided for and had a home in a relatively safe neighborhood. Beyond this the parents had little interaction with the child. They assumed that providing for the child's material needs was adequate. There was little talk in the family home.

Consider another child who was raised by parents who were vitally concerned with the child's feelings. They talked all the time and never ceased wondering how the child felt. Though the parents both worked, the family ate dinner together—during which all people had a chance to talk about their day and express their feelings. In addition, the parents were very interested in having the child continue to college as they both had done. Education was a big deal.

Other people were routinely invited in to the family home, and friends were considered to be important. The child was made to feel welcome in interaction with the friends and was considered an equal in the interactions that occurred.

Another child was raised in a home in which one or both parents were not there. Even when a parent was there, the parent was usually intoxicated or high. All manner of people came and went through the household. In this environment the child was a bit of an afterthought. Routinely ignored, he or she, was largely left to fend for him or herself.

Often there was not enough to eat, and the adults seemed not to care about the food situation. The child witnessed terrifying fights between the adults and also extreme despair that was not soothed in any way. The child spent considerable time on the streets hanging with "friends."

If you meet each one of these three people, a part of understanding them will be to understand the context from which they came.

It is not that they cannot move beyond such a context, but the impact of the context will be noticeable in their interaction patterns.

I learned in my time spent as a psychologist in a public mental health clinic that was placed in the middle of a city that there are people who have never sat in a room with another person and had a conversation. Such behavior seems weird to them.

Talking about themselves seems weird for the same reason. It simply hasn't been done.

More to the point, it is important to get some sense of how a person interacted with his or her parents.

I know a woman who is in her seventies who is still obeying rules set down for her by her father. Though she is rather highly achieved in her life, she still retains the tether to her childhood family rules. She would not think to break them. To her, they are the foundation of her world. They were good before, and they are good now, &c.

Thus, this person has never really left home and discovered by her own efforts who she is. She is still defined by the definitions of her that existed in her childhood family.

It is impossible to understand this person without knowing about her allegiance to family rules. Learning about this is to learn about the context.

Such a situation is akin to a child raised in a strict religious home. Here the rules and ideas of the religion are employed in place of individual reactions. That is reactions are subordinated to the religious ideas.

Such a child learns how to operate in terms prescribed by the religion (at least overtly). He or she does not learn how to operate on his or her own terms. When such a child moves beyond the boundaries of the religion, adaptation to a new context is difficult. He or she will only have religious training upon which to rely.

This person may be said to have an undeveloped or inauthentic sense of self. In the place of a self he or she has a code of behavior or being. Understanding this person requires one to know that fact.

Perhaps the most important factor that may be learned from considering the background context is the possibility or the presence of *trauma*.

Trauma changes everything.

There are three basic forms of trauma: emotional, physical, and sexual.

Each of these leaves psychological scars that influence the behavior of the person who has experienced them. Easily the *most* common of these forms is emotional. The *least* common is sexual trauma.

Emotional trauma presents the additional problem that people who have experienced this do not always realize they have experienced trauma. They may feel their situation was not ideal, but they may never realize it has amounted to trauma and thus requires special consideration.

If there is physical or sexual trauma, there will likely be bruises or some physical sign the trauma has occurred. It will thus make sense what happened. One has been hurt, and there is evidence to show this. Consequently, help may be sought to deal with it.

If the trauma is emotional—and there are no bruises—effects will be much harder to tease out and identify. Help may not be sought, as one thinks that if there are no obvious effects it isn't worth worrying about.

I saw a patient who was an adult professional man whose mother, I learned, was very overpowering, fearful, and demanding. My patient was afraid of almost everything—especially women.

He knew his mother had been a difficult person, but he had no idea of the magnitude of the wounds he had sustained in his interactions with her. It took a great deal of time before this person began to trust me, and even then his interactions were timid and uncertain.

Routinely trauma results in a person who is very sensitive to any danger. Also everything is considered to be a danger until proven otherwise. Trust is routinely slow to establish and can be demolished very easily. "Walking on eggshells" easily describes the experience of being around such people.

It is not uncommon for hurt people to be angry. They may know this or they may not. The anger can take many forms, BUT the people themselves may not realize they are being angry when it is clearly, overtly, the case.

Anger may not have been seen in their background context. It was simply so ubiquitous and so common as to have been considered normal.

Of course no one has come from a perfect context— whatever that might be. Therefore, each person will have dents and bruises left over from earlier experiences. It is wise to consider all dents and bruises important and worthy of compassionate understanding. Our dents and bruises define us as much as do our advantages.

The point is not to judge the past context, but to gain enough access to it to begin to be able to understand it. Once the context is more or less understood, the person who emerged from it will him or herself become more understandable.

We don't choose our childhood circumstances. We don't choose the psychological and emotional capacities of our parents. These things have been approximate for each of us

—sometimes more, sometimes less. It is the only way, if you think about it, we get to be people.

The list of contextual issues could be extended a long way indeed. The point is that one cannot understand another without getting some sense of the context from which he or she came. This is akin to saying it is important to know what experiences the person has had. Asking about details of the context usually provides more clear information than asking about experiences per se. The reason for this, again, is that the person may not realize the impact the context has had.

CHAPTER SIX: MY INPUT/YOUR INPUT

Any interpersonal interaction is a two-way street. This is true in many ways.

There is how I see the situation, and there is how you see the situation.

There is how I feel about it, and how you feel about it.

We both influence each other. You are not the same with me as you are with other people. I am not the same with you as I am with other people. There is an "interaction effect" in play.

In psychoanalysis this issue of how we affect each other in an interaction is called transference and countertransference.

Briefly transference is how you experience me. This includes who you think I am, what you think I am like, how you feel in my presence, how you tend to behave in that situation, and other factors.

Countertransference is how I experience you.

These factors are important, because part of the interaction between us is unique to the present situation. That is, I influence you, and you respond to that influence. You influence me, and I respond to that influence.

The trick is teasing these influences out so they may be understood.

That is, what am I contributing, and what are you contributing?

By far the hardest issue to consider is what I am contributing.

The reason this is so difficult is the difference between an inside view and an outside view. In this sense the person on the outside has an advantage that is compelling. He or she can experience what it is like to be in my presence. That is something I cannot do.

The trick is for me to learn more about what this experience is like. What is it like to be in my presence? Attempting to learn more about this was the reason students of classical psychoanalysis underwent their own psychotherapy. Therapy enabled them to learn more of what it was like to be in their presence—and therefore they were able to see what they were contributing to the interactions they had.

For example, I may be a person who always needs to be in charge. Part of the reactions I get from other people are due to the fact they are responding to this behavior. Knowing I come across like this—whether or not I feel in charge —helps me understand the responses I get from others.

A sense of how I am seen can be obtained from open and honest others, from repeated experience of certain outcomes, or from profoundly intimate interactions. Beyond this psychotherapy is required to learn the intricate and subtle ways I am unwittingly affecting others.

The responses I routinely obtain from others may be due to the fact I only have had one sort of experience. I may, for example, been raised on a farm in a rural area, and I have not been any other place. Thus I do not have all experiences. I only have one experience and the point of view that comes from that experience. I do not have all points of view.

To assume another person will see things the same way I see them is really to assume we had the same history and the same background context. Obviously we didn't. We didn't even if we came from the "same" family.

Parents do not respond to different children the same way. There are subtle as well as profound differences — even if these differences are not clearly apparent on the surface.

If I am going to try to understand a range of other people, I am going to have to shift from my own position and try, as best I can, to see and feel myself into the positions of these others.

It simply will not work for me to wait for these others to come to me. If I want to see and understand them, I must go to them.

For this reason, I must learn as much as possible about the other person so I can shift my perspective to see him or her more adequately. The more I am able to know about him or her, the better I will be able to understand him or her. Still, obviously, I will never be able to completely understand — whatever that might be. "Good enough" understanding will have to suffice.

I may receive the input of another, repeat it to him or her and ask him or her if I have understood it correctly. I may invite corrections from him or her. But, even so, elements of my own will always contaminate my perceptions of the input from another. This is an important thing to keep in mind.

Some of the elements that are exchanged between us in an intimate or therapeutic setting are unconscious. They are present, and influence the interaction, but they are out of sight.

These elements might simply not be known by the person displaying them whereas others may be hidden for an unconscious reason. That is, I may need to be unaware I come across as if I always need to be in charge. If you point this out to me, I may strongly deny it. It is important to my psychological economy that I keep this information out of my own sight.

Such situations are best handled psychotherapeutically. Suffice it to say, there is little gained by "shoving" another's unconscious material down his or her throat. A successful resolution of such an issue requires the mending and repairing of the issues that maintain such behavior.

Material that is available to others but hidden from oneself typically has to do with the self esteem of the person in question. Tearing into another person's self esteem is not the best way to establish intimacy or psychotherapy with him or her.

For our purposes it is sufficient to pay attention to how I tend to affect others, and how others tend to affect me. There is a *pattern* to such interactions. We do them over and over. They are as characteristic of us as is our photograph. Perhaps more so. That is what allows them to be seen and understood.

We say, "Frank is controlling." "Alice is catty."

The ways in which we effect each other give tremendous information about who we are. By observing the effect another person has on me, I am able to learn about him or her. He or she tends to influence people in this way. It is unlikely I am the *only* person he or she affects this way, but that *may* be the case.

It is also the case that, since I am not you—and don't live in your life—I cannot know what you should do. I can tell you what I would do, but that is information that is likely too far away from your circumstance to do much good.

What I can do is try to see and understand the situation as best I can, and help you to have the benefit of that point of view. Since my input will be a different point of view from the one you have now, it may enable you to see the situation differently.

That said, it must be stressed I am a person with my own biases and limitations. These factors will influence the interaction as well. If I don't know what these factors are, it will be measurably more difficult for me to know what I have contributed to the outcome of the interaction.

This is one of the most important arguments in favor of one experiencing his or her own psychotherapy. In this process I will be able to learn more about my own contributions to the interactions I have—and I will be able to learn about these things in a supportive context in which I will be able to tolerate that information.

It is not unusual for us to find ourselves unwittingly playing a part in another person's contextual economy. In a sense we have been *captured* in another's pattern. Once we are so captured, it is as if we are a "pawn in the game." We often lose our independent ability to interact with the person from our own base of integrity.

It is not being caught or trapped that is the problem as such. The problem is not recognizing this and thus ceasing to operate as a genuine other. Therefore, it is incumbent on me to find a way to get *uncaught or untrapped*.

It is the ability to get out of such a predicament that will be new in the other person's experience. And if, say, my therapist can get out, perhaps other people can too. This makes it possible for me to discover a way out of my own traps and context repetitions.

CHAPTER SEVEN: PREPARING YOURSELF FOR SEEING

Clearly any sort of adequate seeing of another requires an openness on one's part.   One must be constantly open to new information and for reformulating one's view of the other.

There are many things that contribute to this "openness to new experience."

Perhaps the most important contributor is to have had a wide range of experiences in many different contexts. Thus going to a place I have never been will allow me to see that things are done differently there.   International travel is such an experience.

As I amass divergent perspectives, it will become clear to me there is no one "correct" perspective.   I will realize what Foucault (1994) suggested: what you see depends upon where you stand.

Also the fact that an inside view and an outside view are different figures heavily here. Rome doesn't look the same from New York City as New York City looks from Rome, &c.

Interacting with many different kinds of people from many different kinds of contexts will also provide a wide experience. We may, for example, go to a widely diverse college in a different context.

Many of us, however, tend to primarily interact with people who are like us and not with people who are not like us. This does not promote breadth of experience.

Lakoff (2016) has summarized the differences between the perceptions of people who are open to new experience and those who are closed.

Basically the difference is this. Openness is cultivated in contexts where what is *outside* the context is of major interest. Every attempt is made to increase one's knowledge and experience of *other* contexts.

Lack of openness, on the other hand, is cultivated in contexts where what is *inside* the context is of major interest. Every attempt is made to increase one's knowledge and experience of the *same* context.

Lakoff said:

> In the strict father family, father knows best. He knows right from wrong and has the ultimate authority to make sure his children and his spouse do what he says, which is taken to be what is right. Many conservative spouses accept this worldview, uphold the father's authority, and are strict in those realms of family life that they are in charge of. When his children disobey, it is his moral duty to punish them painfully enough so that, to avoid punishment, they will obey him (do

what is right) and not just do what feels good. Through physical discipline they are supposed to become disciplined, internally strong, and able to prosper in the external world. What if they don't prosper? That means they are not disciplined, and therefore cannot be moral, and so deserve their poverty. This reasoning shows up in conservative politics in which the poor are seen as lazy and undeserving, and the rich as deserving their wealth. Responsibility is thus taken to be *personal responsibility* not social responsibility. What you become is only up to you; society has nothing to do with it. You are responsible for yourself, not for others — who are responsible for themselves (Ibid).

In such a family context what is able to be experienced is determined by the adult and followed by the child. This is considered ordinary. Not doing this is considered unordinary or abnormal.

Here, it is not necessary to consider other contexts beyond the father's family rule, because either these other contexts are irrelevant or *wrong*. Clearly they are seen as immoral. This present situation is the right context, and other people will either follow the dictates of this context, or they are wrong.

Such an experience stresses that one *get it right*. Right behavior is the goal. It is *not* important for one to *get it real* and be who one really experiences him or herself to be, as that may not be *right*.

Having grown up in such a context it will be difficult for one to relate to significantly different people or to develop any sort of profound intimacy.

Intimacy (of which, again, psychotherapy is a special form) requires an open communication between two *real* persons. If the best I can do is to have an interaction with another person who gets it right, I can't move close enough for intimacy to occur.

This is a critical point.

If I am standing firm on my own position (the *right* position) I will not allow myself to move into the space of another to get a view from that person's perspective—for the obvious reason that, if they differ from me, they are clearly wrong. Thus, I will miss certain understandings of them.

In order for any sort of significant intimacy or psychotherapy to occur, two real selves must meet, greet each other, and interact.

There are two further consequences of the strict family described by Lakoff.

> The strict father logic extends further. The basic idea is that authority is justified by morality (the strict father version), and that, in a well-ordered world, there should be

(and traditionally has been) a moral hierarchy in which those who have traditionally dominated *should* dominate. The hierarchy is: God above Man, Man above Nature, The Disciplined (Strong) above the Undisciplined (Weak), The Rich above the Poor, Employers above Employees, Adults above Children, Western culture above other cultures, America above other countries. The hierarchy extends to: Men above women, Whites above Nonwhites, Christians above non-Christians, Straights above Gays (Ibid).

In such a situation it will be difficult for people to switch roles as there is a moral reason to maintain one's own role. Shifting roles may be considered improper.

Another issue is as follows:

Direct causation is dealing with a problem via direct action. Systemic causation recognizes that many problems arise from the system they are in and must be dealt with via systemic causation. Systemic causation has four versions: A chain of direct causes. Interacting direct causes (or chains of direct causes). Feedback loops. And probabilistic causes (Ibid).

The difference here may be thought of as the difference between simple and complex explanations. In a simple explanation one factor is assumed to account for the result. In complex explanations many factors are seen to be involved.

In strict systems, simple causation tends to be favored. In open systems, complex causation tends to be favored.

What these views are suggesting is that an open view is far more effective in the areas of intimacy and psychotherapy than is a closed view.

Any sort of adequate seeing of another person requires an open and flexible attitude, so one is able to move around and adjust one's perspective when it is required.

Interestingly, this can prove to be a problem to those who are trained and heavily invested in a formal scientific point of view. Being overly scientific can be akin to being rigid.

In Chapter Two I quoted O'Connor (1960) as describing a move beyond strict or rigid forms of understanding in favor of an attitude of exploration of what can never be completely known—what she calls the mystery.

It is commonly said that psychoanalysts pride themselves on not knowing anything. This allows them to be constantly open to new understandings and the search for those understandings from multiple sources.

In order to prepare oneself for seeing, the widest and most open perspectives possible must be sought. It is only by breadth of experience and viewpoints that a complex view is possible.

Since both intimacy and psychotherapy seek an understanding of another person, complexity is what the search is about—because another person will be an extremely complex being.

There is no right way to see another person. Nor is there a right way to be a person.

In intimacy and in psychotherapy the task is different. In these enterprises the task is to *find* the other person. That is the task is to move around among contexts and feelings until one finds resonance with the other.

This sort of experience is like standing in the same place or seeing the same thing. It is that which profoundly erases isolation and aloneness.

It is the experience of finding the other person that increases his or her trust in the enterprise. It is also likely the first time anyone found him or her in an empathic and accepting way. This experience itself profoundly deepens the interaction and opens new avenues for seeing and understanding.

CHAPTER EIGHT: SEEING BEYOND DEFENSES

An obstacle to adequately seeing and understanding an-other person has to do with the use of psychological de-fenses.

Defenses are ways in which people keep themselves from things that cause them undue anxiety. These defenses may be employed either consciously or unconsciously and may be either simple or complex.

For example, imagine a person who is constantly appear-ing to be in charge, capable, and important. A casual expe-rience of this person is that he or she knows what they are doing and is adequate.

Let us assume for a moment this person has a secret. This is: he or she at a deep level actually feels inadequate and has erected the complex appearance of seeming to be in charge, capable, and important in order to keep her secret hidden.

Imagine further that in intimacy or in psychotherapy it is suggested that *behind* the person's appearance as being all capable, he or she really feels inadequate. That is, his or her secret is discovered by another.

Upon hearing this the person strongly *denies* it is true. He or she may be offended or become angry it has been suggested.

This is the use of a defense. It is the defense of *denial*. The person does not admit this is the case if he or she knows of its existence, or refuses to acknowledge it, because he or she has unwittingly kept it unaware.

It is also an instance of what is called *reaction formation*, that is presenting what is the opposite of the actual case.

The problem of course is that if one is in a relationship with another person and learns things about the other person that he or she denies or disowns, a conflict between them may occur.

That is seeing may go beyond a person's awareness.

In order to maintain the relationship with another, a person may elect to *pretend* he or she does *not* see or feel the things that have been discovered—and simply go on as before but with a restricted range of interaction.

If many people in that person's environment also pretend to not see or know the denied information, these people may be said to be *colluding* in a kind of interpersonal psychological plot, namely to keep the information out of sight.

No one around here speaks about grandma's drinking problem.

The psychological term for this situation is that it is a *dysfunctional relationship*. A dysfunctional relationship is one in which there are truths that must be denied or kept secret in order to keep the relationship functioning and intact.

The discovering of defenses is routine in psychotherapy. Therefore, if awareness of the defended material cannot be tolerated by the patient, the therapist may temporarily accept the use of the defense as he or she tries to build up the ego strength of the patient.

Once the ego strength of the patient is adequate, he or she will be able to acknowledge the denied information.

It is important to stress we as people have defenses for a reason. They keep us from becoming overwhelmed. In understood and reasonable use, defenses are *normal*.

Defenses can become problematical, however, if they are *overused* or relied upon *exclusively*.

Also a significant problem may occur when both people have similar defenses. Both may be products of environments in which certain information was not allowed. Thus when one person withholds information, the other may simply consider this to be normal—and therefore miss the fact it is a defense.

This is a problem in psychotherapy as it is impossible to help the other to develop a more successful coping strategy if the defense is not recognized and understood.

It is important to recognize the defense is doing important psychological work—or the energy required to maintain it would not make sense. Ripping away defenses does *not* improve the situation. Taking them away before the person is able to tolerate what the defenses have masked leaves the person *worse* off than before. At least before (with the defense) he or she could function. Now he or she is incapable.

Both cruel people and inadequate therapists are famous for a desire to destroy defenses without considering the consequences.

Defenses may become a problem in intimacy when the relationship is established on a dysfunctional basis. Thus the relationship consists of people who have significant secrets to be kept from the other. If, in the course of time and development, one person develops the capacity to move beyond his or her defense, the other person may find him or herself in a relationship in which his or her own defense is more vulnerable.

Jane may decide to stop denying grandma's drinking problem. She may want to talk about it and do something.

This can disrupt the psychological balance of the relationship. When areas that were off limits suddenly become legitimate topics of discussion (or vice versa), new relationship adjustments must be made.

This dilemma is a constant factor in psychotherapy when one member of a couple seeks psychotherapy, and the other does not.

As the member in psychotherapy begins to resolve his or her issues, material that was hidden or not noticed becomes available. That is to say the patient is now able to see from a different perspective. New things may be noticed and realized.

This change of perspective will affect the person's intimate relationship, simply because there is more information to share. The person is no longer the same, having grown in understanding and capability.

The partner not in treatment is suddenly faced with a different person with whom to interact. A whole new sort of relationship may be required to manage this situation.

Worse, the patient, having discovered his or her new information, may be able to see information the other partner is hiding—information, further, which the other would just as soon not recognize, thank you.

This situation is related to the notion of *levels of seeing*. As a rule, relationships exist between people at similar levels of seeing. It is unusual for significant mismatch to occur within couples, families, or networks of friends. This is the reason post graduate students are routinely not intimate partners with high school drop-outs.

Also it is the case we ignore defenses in polite company as we typically try to keep the pond as smooth as possible in the service of furthering pleasant discussions and outcomes. This is often the case in work environments where congeniality is often more important than truth. (Sometimes, however, it is not.)

Developing good social skills requires a capacity to interact easily with different kinds of people who have different abilities. Such pleasantry may quickly become a problem in intimacy and in psychotherapy where a more complete and more honest interaction is sought.

In a society like we have there is no "one size fits all" solution. Intimacy and psychotherapy are extreme examples of openness. Typically work relationships are less open. The people we meet on the street are even less open.

The capacity to see and understand others is related to *bandwidth*. This is a measure of how much a person can see. Some of us have rather narrow bandwidths. Others have wide abilities.

If we are going to see each other, it will be necessary that our bandwidths be wide enough to include the dimensions of the other person, otherwise important factors will be beyond view and not seen.

A society is only as capable as its shared bandwidth will allow. For similar reasons, it is wise for therapists to expand their bandwidths as far as possible. In this way more people may be adequately seen and helped.

CHAPTER NINE: PROBLEMS IN SEEING

There are several places where adequate seeing is difficult if not impossible. In these areas one's seeing is distorted in ways he or she may not realize.

For example, it is difficult to get a clear picture of someone whose life-context is radically different from one's own. His or her experience is simply too far away.

There are things one can do in this situation to get closer, but it is likely there will always be significant gaps in one's seeing that will render it approximate at best.

The obvious example concerns people from another *culture*, one you have not contacted before. Trying to see such persons in terms of one's own culture will likely result in misreading that may be important.

This point will become clear to someone who has traveled widely, yet, even so, disparities will remain.

Most of us are trained to see what is in our context. Consequently, we can only *imagine* the things we have not seen. The uneducated cannot easily find the educated. A non-artistic person cannot easily find an artistic person. A rich person cannot easily find a poor person. A poor person cannot easily find a rich person. Who can find the Little

Match Girl (Andersen, 2001)?

Oddly enough another problem is trying to see someone who is very much like you.

This is a problem as the other will be very much like one and yet different in important ways. Such differences may be difficult to tease out in the presence of so much that is similar.

Of course these comments concern contexts. People from different contexts will be different. And when the seeing gets especially close, *everyone* will be seen to be from a different context. Thus at an extremely close level, no two people have experienced the *same* context—important micro-differences apply. Lumping people together in categories or groups may be beneficial for some purposes, but it is likely to be a dramatic problem in others.

Another area where seeing may be problematical concerns age. The age of a person clearly demonstrates different contexts of origin. Contexts constantly change over time, as do the people who live within them.

This can be seen clearly in the way much adolescent music and lingo shifts over time. It is important that these things are different from the music and lingo of the parents, who now have become the old generation. This indicates a break in the continuity of experience. It helps adolescents separate from their parents and the parents' contexts.

Having practically spent my whole life in universities, it is fascinating to see how the "scene" constantly shifts over time.   Attitudes change, clothes change, points of view change, what matters and what does not changes, &c.

Tuning into the rhythms of a generation other than one's own will always be approximate, and one will inevitably end up with a "foreign accent."

This is why so many parents, teachers, politicians, and other "old fogies" just don't get it.

On the other hand, it is somewhat automatic on one's part to make assumptions about different age groups.   One is only able to see what one knows.   For example, children's abilities to grasp and understand things are routinely under-estimated.   The wisdom of older people is constantly over-estimated.

These issues will be true of each person.   Others will make assumptions about one.   These assumptions may include biases as well as views that do not fit one's position very well—or at all.

The sheer amount of confusion that can occur between perspectives, judgment, and assumptions is enough to de-rail many honest attempts to see and understand.

Stereotypes apply.   People who work in the corporate world are assumed to possess a certain chipper compliance with the system.   People with beards and long hair are often considered shiftless.

Such perceptions *may* be true in general, but there will be significant differences left over by such views.

And, of course, in our own time the issues of gender and sexuality have become significantly complex.

It is important to move beyond rigid conceptions of gender and sexuality in order to understand people as anything other than stereotypes. It *MAY* be the case a person has been trained to fit into rigid stereotypes of gender instead of being who they really discover themselves to be—categories aside. But it is also possible the person *HAS NOT* been so conditioned.

Not all women like flowers; not all men like football.

It is only by considering the genuine thoughts and feelings of individuals that some sense of how they see themselves in terms of gender and sexuality may be formulated.

This issue is obviously at play with regard to the LGBTQI community where an unaccepting attitude will be quickly discovered. For therapists this spells disaster. It places a judgment in the way of adequate seeing and understanding.

On the other hand, forms of different sexuality and gender identity may be so alien to one's own experience as to be virtually incomprehensible. In such cases it behooves one to learn more about these areas before trying to seriously see and understand them.

In the case of psychotherapy personal judgment rarely has a place anyway. Whether or not the therapist likes and approves of a patient is an issue of the therapist not of the patient. It is also clearly an issue for the therapist's own supervision or psychotherapy.

People don't seek psychotherapy to be judged.

Other seeing difficulties center around differences in socio-economic status, educational status, and individual ability, to name a few.

A special difficulty is encountered when the other is significantly brighter, more capable, and/or more accomplished than one. That is, the other person's bandwidth easily outpaces one's own.

One's self esteem may suffer. This may either be unconscious or conscious. For example, I may do everything I can to try to convince you of my own qualities. I may even find myself trying to minimize you.

I may find myself in awe of you. I may not see qualities in you that matter as I can only respond to your superiority.

Any of these things may derail an adequate sense of seeing and understanding. My own issues may be in the way. It may only be possible for me to discover this in my own psychotherapy or supervision.

Related to this is a problem each of us share that is known in the psychological literature as "self-confirming bias." In such a situation I tend to find evidence from my perceptions and experience that my views are as correct as I thought they were.

This is the ability to look out and obtain proof the world is exactly the place I thought it was. I always find I am right.

Such a finding is actually quite easy to obtain. The trick, as any psychotherapist will tell you, is to be able to look out and obtain proof the world is *not* the place you thought it was. That is a *hard* perception to achieve.

In experimental psychology, for example, investigators are routinely conducting "objective" experiments and obtaining data that *confirm* their hypotheses. This may involve a bias known as the Rosenthal Effect (See Rosenthal, 2009). It is simply the case that subtle issues regularly influence our perceptions so that we see what we want to see.

In fact, it is difficult to do otherwise—and seeing otherwise typically requires significant training and wide ranging experience.

A safe position is to assume one's perceptions are biased and work from there, trying to find evidence for bias and make sense of it. This is hard to do as we typically most forcefully defend the views we have that are most suspect. It is healthy and wise to constantly be on the alert for evidence that will indicate one's own views are contaminated in ways one may not grasp.

Each of these issues demonstrates the need on one's part to look harder, listen harder, and keep an open mind for new information. No understanding is ever the final word. People and contexts are constantly evolving and shifting.

What is seen today will not likely be seen in the same way tomorrow.

A patient of mine who was a professor of physics told me it is a consequence of the equations worked out by Einstein that there is no known thing in the universe that is static. Everything is in motion; everything changes.

An enormous benefit of one experiencing his or her own psychotherapy is that one is able to become acquainted with one's own biases, blind spots, and shortcomings. In light of such discoveries events in one's life begin to make sense, and one is able to understand oneself in a new sense. This is remarkably akin to *having a new life*. The experience of being able to see from different perspectives is wide-sweeping and profound.

It is not wise for one to shrink away from the opportunity to obtain such information about oneself. On the contrary, it is what allows one to see most clearly.

CHAPTER TEN: SACRED GROUND

Some qualities and characteristics are extremely subtle and/or personal and are therefore very difficult to see and understand.

Just as the musical sounds that are *beyond* one's ability to hear interact with and thus color the sounds one *is* able to hear within a defined space, what is *not* seen and understood in any situation interacts with that which *is* seen and understood—and colors it in similar fashion.

In psychology (social psychology) intimacy is routinely thought of in terms of *proximate space*. This is much like an "onion rings theory." Thus the outer ring represents people we simply pass by, say, on the street and know nothing about. The next ring comprises those we recognize but know little or nothing about. At the next ring are people we see frequently and recognize. At the next ring are people with whom we interact politely, i.e. we say "Hi."

Finally, we get to the level of intimacy where both ourselves and the other try to be as open and available to each other as possible. This is also the situation that exists in significant psychotherapy.

The most extreme level of intimacy may be held to concern what issues matter to a person more than any other thing. This may be something (or some things) that one never or rarely talks about. It is too personal, too private.

Such personal issues form what is sacred ground to a person. They are the things "without which not." They may be more important than life itself. They are, in any event, the source of great personal reverence.

These kinds of issues cannot be assumed from the outside. What is sacred to one person may or may not be sacred to another. In fact, what is sacred to one will likely differ in meaningful ways from what is sacred to another.

For example, a close friend of mine, with whom I was an undergraduate student at the university, had a developed interest in the "same" kind of music that I have. We could listen to the "same" music, and both enjoy it tremendously. I dare say, however, we didn't have the *same* experience. Our experiences were *similar*, maybe closely so, but *similar* nonetheless.

It is obvious why this would be the case. Each of us came from different contexts and lived in different contexts. Though we were and remain extremely close, important differences remain.

When I speak of sacred ground, I do *not* mean to allude to organized religion. What is sacred is simply that which matters greatly. It has a powerful personal significance. This *may* be organized religion, but it *need* not be.

In fact, it probably doesn't have much to do with organized religion at all. It may be a person. It may be a memory. It may be some thing. It may be a work of art. It may be a kind of seeing and feeling. It may even be a street.

What is sacred is that which means the most, a thing, dimension, or person from which I obtain significant "meaning" and depth.

Further, things that are held to be sacred are approached and considered with a kind of humility. This is important as humility is a state that is open and receptive.

Being sacred, and meaning that much to me, I do not routinely share such space with everyone. I don't do this as it is not likely such a thing, dimension, or person will be sacred to them—let alone even understood. It will not have the depth it has for me. It may mean nothing to them. Another person may stomp all over it, and I would just as soon avoid that.

It is for this reason sacred issues are usually private. One may not have found others, or another, who have be able to hold such things without mockery. Children routinely withhold such information from their parents, for example—and forget one's school peers.

I share what is sacred to me only when I feel another will be able to treat it with the proper respect and reverence. Such matters are fragile in a way. They demand care.

For these reasons discovering what is sacred ground for another is an act of extreme intimacy. In a sense it is the most a person can offer. And for this reason it may be the element that allows for the most complete seeing and understanding of that person. It is, as it were, to know them at their "core."

Hart Crane (1958) wrote:

My Grandmother's Love Letters

There are no stars tonight
But those of memory.
Yet how much room for memory there is
In the loose girdle of soft rain.

There is even room enough
For the letters of my mother's mother,
Elizabeth,
That have been pressed so long
Into a corner of the roof
That they are brown and soft,
And liable to melt as snow.

Over the greatness of such space
Steps must be gentle.
It is all hung by an invisible white hair.
It trembles as birch limbs webbing the air.

And I ask myself:

"Are your fingers long enough to play
Old keys that are but echoes:
Is the silence strong enough

To carry back the music to its source
And back to you again
As though to her?"

Yet I would lead my grandmother by the hand
Through much of what she would not understand;
And so I stumble. And the rain continues on the roof
With such a sound of gently pitying laughter.

Gentle steps indeed.

CHAPTER ELEVEN: LOVE

Closely related to sacred ground is love. In fact, love may be *the* sacred ground.

There are several issues related to the experience of love in terms of intimacy and psychotherapy. At the outset it must be stressed that love involves a profound set of feelings. These color the perceptions one has.

It is an old saying: love is blind.

There is a difference between the intense experience of "falling in love" and the experience of a deep emotional and physical connection that is enduring and profound.

This difference is akin to the levels of seeing and understanding. Falling in love is discovering that two people have the same attracted feelings for each other. It is a heady experience and typically takes first place in one's priority system.

Projective identification figures in this kind of attraction. I transfer my adoration *into* another person, and he or she transfers his or her adoration *into* me. Thus we discover we have the *same* feelings for each other.

These are feelings beyond those we have for others. These feelings are intense, pleasant, and euphoric. We feel we have met someone unique.

The problem with this experience is that it is far from an objective view. To put it mildly. It is an experience colored by our hopes and longings. It is filled with everything we have been looking for. There are few experiences in life quite so exciting—or, sometimes, quite so disturbing.

As our time with this other person with whom we are in love continues, we begin to notice things that are not so ideal. But, we say, those are few and not very significant— next to all that is so good and right.

As time goes further on, we begin to notice more things that are not so ideal. In fact, we soon learn that this "perfect" other is not so perfect after all. In fact they are, as we are, a flawed human being.

This realization may or may not matter in terms of the health and continuation of the relationship. That is, it is at this point that the opportunity opens to deepen the relationship in a significant way.

The person may have become dear to me in spite of his or her shortcomings. I may be able to embrace his or her shortcomings as I embrace the person him or herself. This in turn may lead to new and deeper levels of intimacy and understanding.

I may not be able to tolerate my discovery of things that are not perfect in another and move to end the relationship.

Thus I begin to seek another person who I feel will be more suitable as a partner. This search may be more or less successful.

I may, however, find that what I cannot tolerate is imperfection in any form and thus choose to remain single.

Love, again, involves sexual feelings and behavior. It is an intimacy that *includes* sexuality. Psychotherapy, on the other hand, is an intimacy that *excludes* sexuality.

Both are areas where we slowly become more known to another and in which another becomes more known to us.

Along the way in both situations there are numerous areas in which a more or less clear view becomes impeded. Defenses, personal psychological issues, &c. get in the way.

For this reason, most couples develop some form of compromised intimacy and have areas that have been declared "off limits." This itself is not lethal to the relationship. It may be a worked out compromise that serves the relationship in a positive way.

But the issue that is much more troubling to an intimacy is the presence of secrets. *These can become lethal to the relationship.*

The reason for this is simply that secrets tend to interfere with the openness required to maintain a working intimacy. They, therefore, work as a "withholding of openness" factor which itself is not seen or discussed. When such a situation is discovered it is difficult not to hold the person responsible for damaging the openness assumption, and the relationship suffers accordingly.

Related to these matters are people who, in searching for love, have lists of qualities an acceptable partner must have. This is akin to a shopping list to take to the market.

When such a person meets another, this other is compared to the list one has—and is either accepted or rejected on these terms.

People with detailed lists are examples of persons who don't really know what a relationship is.

A working relationship is an interaction between two persons in which individual selves are offered and interact with each other. In a sense, it is the interior that is shared as much as the activity. One can share activities with someone with whom one is not intimate.

Finding someone with similar interests leads to an adjacency for sure, but it may not move beyond that to the development of intimacy. This is also true of someone who "looks right," that is fits one's specification for what an ideal partner might look like.

Intimacy is intimacy. It is established by the meeting of selves, not the meeting of lists or external traits (beauty, wealth, &c.).

Also there is simply no way a relationship *should* be.

Intimate relationships are constructed by two people who are in the business of discovering what is necessary for each one to willingly continue in the interaction.

It is as if two people get together, put all their important desires on a table, and then stand there wondering what can be done with all that stuff.

What can be done with it is something *both* people must decide and accept. Only in this way will both people be able to get behind the effort to make the relationship work.

Some of the elements may not be ideal, but none of them can be deal-breakers. The resulting relationship may be an odd looking sort of affair that works for the people involved but may not work for anyone else. It may look weird indeed to others, but it works for the people involved. That is the point.

Related to this issue is the almost universal fear of rejection.

There are many dear people who feel isolated and wish they could reach out to potential partners and friends, but the fear that the other won't be interested keeps them bound in a paralyzing fear.

I have found these people have not thought through what "reaching out" involves. *It does not involve a test of one's quality or desirability as a human being.*

Reaching out really asks a simple question. "What are your circumstances?"

The other person may be appealing for a number of reasons, but one doesn't know what this other is like as a person. Reaching out is designed to solve this equation.

The other may say, "Hi, I'm glad to meet you too."

The other may say, "Drop dead, you jerk."

It is simply not the case that the first answer shows I am a desirable human being, while the second answer shows I am a lowly toad.

In fact—*and this is the point*—the answer says more about the *other* person that it does about oneself.

How I respond to others is a quality of *mine*. It is not a quality of someone who says "Hi" to me.

The act of reaching out asks whether another is willing or able to be friendly, to chat, perhaps to have coffee, and perhaps to want to get to know more about one. It is important to keep reaching out at this level.

It can be done with anyone, even check-out clerks.

At any rate "No" most certainly does not mean I am now relegated forever and evermore to the pile of sad, hopeless losers who are too hideous to ever find someone to be kind to them.

At the other end of things, it may be time to leave a relationship when one can no longer stay in the relationship and be truthful to him or herself. That is to say the relationship may have become too limited in some way for one to continue without severely distorting who he or she is.

Actually, before one leaves, this is a good time to consult a competent therapist who can avoid taking sides. Such a person can listen to each person's positions and help him or her to find acceptable options. It is not for a therapist to decide what should happen or whose view is better.

If one person simply cannot be in the relationship any longer, that is the reality of the situation.

On the other hand, the person who is most distraught as well as his or her partner may be able to develop new insights and perspectives to make it possible and even desirable to continue.

Being accepted in spite of one's flaws is a powerful experience that is routinely life changing. As a rule, such a situation has not happened before.

It requires a degree of maturity as well as mental health to be able to accept one's shortcomings and still retain a healthy working sense of self esteem.

In this regard guilt and shame may play a part in one's feelings. For example, one may be afraid to enter or leave a relationship, because he or she would feel guilty or ashamed. (I am not good enough to say "Hi" to him.) (If I leave her, she will be miserable and heartbroken.)

Guilt and shame, however, are not good bases for relationships. Psychologists typically describe guilt as a reaction to something one did or did not do. Shame, on the other hand, is a quality of the self. The difference is between doing something bad versus being bad.

The discovery in oneself of these emotions is a good time to consult a therapist. One also might do this if he or she feels that hugely inferior people are always saying "Hi" or if one's heart is broken forever, because a relationship didn't work out.

Since intimate relationships involve us at our deepest levels, it is here that interpersonal problems will likely appear first. When one experiences a significant disturbance in one's love life or sex life, this is typically an indication something is not working in the intimacy itself.

The quest to be seen is the quest to be loved. In this sense the inner life *is* life.

Love can be the greatest human experience. It is important to give it every chance.

CHAPTER TWELVE: EMPATHY

At the center of every instance of intimacy and psychotherapy lies empathy. It involves a kind of seeing and comprehending like no other.

The difference between empathy and compassion is this. Compassion is *feeling for.* Empathy is *feeling with.*

Thus in intimacy it may be said we are able to have each other's feelings in a sense. We feel it too.

In a way empathy allows the "inside" thoughts and feelings to be considered. Without empathy, there is only surface observation—the outside.

This can easily be seen in parents' interactions with their children. If the parent is capable of empathy, the focus will be on the child's thoughts and feelings. If empathy is not present, the only focus can be on the child's behavior.

The result may be a well behaved child who is nonetheless not heard and not emotionally included (see Gill, 2015).

Further, it is often in childhood a person learns that interactions between people either can or cannot include empathy.

Of course not all interactions are able to include empathy. Many of our interactions are simple transactions that do not require nor do they invite empathy.

When it comes to intimacy, however, empathy is the essential ingredient. It is this capacity that allows us to get close together and feel together. Intimacy includes the experience of feeling as if you are one with another in an important sense.

Without empathy there is a gap or distance in the interaction. In a sense without empathy we tend to treat each other as objects not as subjects with a human side.

In fact, when there are problems in a relationship, lack of empathy is frequently to blame. We lose touch with another's thoughts and feelings, or we simply don't care about them.

Much talk in relationships concerns attempts to establish, reinforce, or repair empathy. We tell each other what we think and how we feel. It is how we maintain closeness.

In psychotherapy similar concerns apply.

Certainly there are forms of psychotherapy that operate without empathy. Behaviorism and its multiple variants are an example (i.e., empathy is not essential).

Much psychotherapy, however, requires the presence of a working relationship. This is the case as the kinds of problems with which psychotherapy deals have typically occurred and risen within relationships. The issue is that the problems occurred in problematical or troubled relationships.

It makes sense that the solution will be found in a different kind of (i.e., more healthy) relationship.

In fact, many problems are patterns and behaviors that were considered normal in their original environments. It was the environments that were abnormal—often the entire set of interactions.

A person with such a problem has to learn to interact in a different kind of environment (i.e., one that is healthier).

Needless to say this requires a therapist who knows what a healthier kind of environment is. The therapist need not be a paragon of perfect mental health him or herself—indeed no therapist is—but the therapist needs to know what that is. He or she also needs to know how far he or she differs from that position.

That being said, it is necessary that the therapist be able to establish an empathic attunement with the patient. This is so, because much of the therapy will involve exploration and management of intimate thoughts and feelings.

If the therapist is not capable of empathy, it is likely the patient will not be able to "open up" to any significant degree. That is, the patient won't be able to allow the therapist a close orientation.

Empathy tends to beget empathy. Distance tends to beget distance.

This has become a problem in psychotherapy as much recent psychological emphasis has been on technique instead of being on relationships.

Coupled with this is a concern about personal and sexual improprieties in psychotherapy.

Certainly these concerns are legitimate. Psychotherapy is a form of intimacy that excludes sexual behavior. Psychotherapy includes only talk. This is its virtue. Were sexual behavior to occur, the interaction would cease to be psychotherapy. The necessary boundaries would not exist.

Out of intense fear of such interactions, many therapists have become increasingly distant and formal in their interactions with patients. This is unfortunate and unnecessary.

This is not to say that behavior *per se* lies outside the realm of psychotherapy. It is the case that psychotherapy concerns the thoughts, feelings, and origins of such behavior. It can also include the contingency patterns that maintain the behavior.

Rigid distance in psychotherapy limits the information that is allowed to be considered. Just as I will be able to move closer to better see and understand someone with whom I am intimate than I will be able to do with someone I simply meet in an elevator, so in psychotherapy an intimate position enhances effectiveness.

Part of the reason this is true is that problem thoughts and feelings often developed in a person in response to distancing contexts and compromised persons—often parents.

Being able to experience a close, caring interaction that does *not* include the problem distortions and compromises can be an important element in resolving the problem.

Sooner or later every patient says, "Nobody hears me." (Nobody *really* hears me.)

Since this is the case it is incumbent on the therapist to attempt to *really* see and hear. This cannot be done at a distance—but no boundaries need be crossed to do this. All that is required is that the therapist genuinely sees and feels what the patient is presenting.

For this reason, it is often the case that the most significant boundary violation in psychotherapy is *too much distance.* In order to be super-compliant, the therapist simply does not allow him or herself to move any closer.

Empathic resonance is a situation where there is an emotional attunement between two people. That is, they are both feeling the same thing or are participating in the same feeling. This is the height of intimacy. It is usually a profound experience that dwarfs all others.

Empathic resonance allows my views of you and your views of me to meet in the middle, as it were. That is, our views are able to connect. This is akin to what the analyst Thomas Ogden (2001) called "the analytic third."

When our views can connect in this way we are able to correct facets of the other's view that don't match our own experience, and vice versa.

For example, a very sweet patient of mine said one day that she felt she was "an abomination."

I was floored! Nothing could be farther from the truth. I would be surprised if anyone thought this except the patient herself. But that was the view she accepted as correct, and, as a result, that was the view that affected her self image and interactions with others.

She never would have told me this if she did not feel safe and also felt that at some level I would understand the conflict inherent in that view.

As time went on in our treatment I was able to see that this person's father had been a harsh and depressed man who had no encouraging words for his child. The experience stuck.

There are other situations in which empathy is not employed in the service of relating.

Intense competition is such a place. Here the goal is not understanding so much as winning. Empathy may be employed to help me understand more about my competitors, but winning is the goal.

A life that is more or less entirely made up of competition, however, will tend to be an empty life. There is an old saying that those who are good at home are not so good in business, whereas those good in business are not so good at home.

There is a kernel of truth in this statement as the two domains typically require different skills.

It is also possible to compartmentalize competition and empathic relating or intimacy into different sectors. While this is possible, it is a large requirement. Nonetheless it can be accomplished, and may be a goal worth seeking in the sense that it is required in complex contexts.

Empathic seeing is more common in people who have had a secure attachment history than those who have not. This is obvious as empathic seeing is a crucial element in feeling one belongs.

Securely attached people, in an important sense, have experienced empathy all their lives. The rest of us have to learn this ability along the way. Both the experience of intimacy and psychotherapy are important ways to learn this.

What the above suggests is that there is a significant difference between empathic seeing and simply seeing. Empathic seeing is closer. It concerns dimensions beyond a surface look.

Both intimacy and psychotherapy occur within that space beyond a surface look. These are experiences that include the whole person, both surface and depth dimensions. As such the whole person is welcomed and helped to feel safe.

CHAPTER THIRTEEN: TEENAGE REBELLION

If there is one group that is routinely seen in a negative light it is teenagers who rebel. Still, if you think about it, rebels become effective to the degree they know how to target their rebellion most effectively.

To state the obvious, rebels are *angry*. In order to see and understand them, this anger must be understood.

Another obvious point is that in order for there to be a rebellion, there must be something to rebel *against*. It is routinely the case that the rebellion is directed against the parents and their rule system.

It is easy for rebellion to rise and take root in homes where there is a strict father type of system in place. In this environment, the parents issue the rules for the family and see that they are enforced. This is usually done with sufficient force to frighten the child into compliance.

There also may be an overcontrolling mother who seeks to mold the child in her image, demanding compliance.

But frightening or controlling the child is not all that happens. The child learns that if one is in charge he or she can order others around or decide his or her own fate. If one is not in charge one can only obey. Those in charge have a voice. Those not in charge do not.

The inevitable result of being denied an effective voice—or being "done to"—is anger. This anger grows. When the child reaches adolescence he or she discovers that, being bigger, he or she is beginning to have a sense of him or herself as an effective person. Action is now possible that would not have been possible before.

Teenagers also learn their behavior matters to their parents—who may want to maintain the appearance of a successful and happy family. Acting out in the form of physical or sexual activities has a high potential to disturb such a rosy view.

Also the peer group in school consists of others who have unhearing and problem parents as well, and these other students are also angry. The teenager finds him or herself in welcome company of those who feel aggrieved and disenfranchised.

Routinely the goal of these groups is to do the *opposite* of what they are told. How hard is that? This has a very desirable effect. It makes adults angry. This is an amazing discovery of *power*. The tables have been turned: now the teenagers are doing things to the adults. Amazing.

To make things worse, rebellious teenagers are routinely dealt with by the use of punishment and force. Autocratic systems including those in schools and police forces are often eager to mete out condemnation and punishment.

Even if an attempt is made to understand the adolescent, the understanding person must find a way to gain the teen's *trust*. Certainly most if not all the adults in the teenager's past have used listening as a trick in order to find further ways to create compliance.

Trust is created when another person "gets it." That is, another person understands the rebellion as well as the forces that gave rise to it.

The amount of anger exhibited by the teenager is likely the *same level* of anger or force that he or she feels he or she received from parents and other "authorities."

If, however, a person or a therapist can welcome and tolerate the resistance and anger displayed by the teenager, he or she will be seen as behaving in a new way—a way the teenager has likely not found before.

Such a person or therapist must however continue to realize that this teenaged person is very wounded and bears what will likely be lifelong scars related to the time in their childhood when they were treated as an object—to fit into the family system—when the adolescent's feelings were ignored.

If you take away one's voice, you take away his or her dignity.

Teenage rebels are masters at the art of opposition. This is to be expected. In a sense, it is what they have been (often unwittingly) *trained* to do. This is true, because if you think about it, resisting and rebelling are the only ways the adolescent could retain even shards of being a person. If he or she had complied, he or she would have become a thing. A complaint object.

We had a saying at my hospital which was: "The bad kid is never the real kid."

Of course the good kid is never the real kid either. The only real kid is the *whole* kid, good parts, bad parts, and those in-between.

People who are raised in families in which they are taught to fit in and follow the prescribed plan learn how to follow plans. They do *not* as a rule learn how to stand on their own feet and attempt to solve problems. They only know how to apply approved approaches and behaviors.

Further, they learn no one will listen to them, and certainly no one will try to help.

Rules can essentially omit persons.

In such homes thoughts and feelings are not routinely considered. This leaves only behavior as a focal point. When the only thing that matters to parents is how the child behaves, *who* the child is becomes lost.

The other people the child encounters are simply assumed to be similar to parents and teachers—until clearly proven otherwise. This may be all the adolescent has ever known.

Parents of rebellious teenagers are typically similar to the teenagers, except they formulate and attempt to enforce rules for compliance instead of rebelling against those rules. No one sees or hears anyone.

There are many ways to not listen to another.

I recently stopped for coffee at a shop where a mother and an adorable little boy came in and sat close to me. The mother then busied herself with her phone and ignored the little boy. He was bored. When she got up to get herself some coffee (nothing for the boy), he got up and joined her.

She sent him back to his seat.

He climbed up on the seat and gave a frustrated sigh. He glanced at me, and I made a kind of frustrated face too.

After that, he kept checking on me. Presently he took a banana out of his backpack and put it on the counter. I raised my eyebrows in a gesture of "wow!" He offered a slight smile.

After a little time had passed and mother had come back to her phone, he reached in his backpack, got out a package of some sort of snack, and held it out to me as an offer.

I declined with a smile, and yet I was very touched. A total stranger had made contact with this boy whom his mother had not (had not, at least, on this occasion). It was so easy. All I had to do was treat him like a person.

Autocratic parents typically didn't invent such a pattern all by themselves. They routinely had parents who treated them in the same, or similar, ways they treat their own children. It passes along "unto the seventh generation,"

Nurturing parents also likely came from nurturing homes themselves or have done significant personal work on their own psychology. This too passes along.

But the most important thing that can be done with children is to *see* them and *hear* them. If they have to do something they don't want to do, that can be heard and understood—even if they have to do it.

Then they understand that others understand how much it sucks to have to do this thing. The child is no longer alone. The parent is able to share in the feeling.

When my son Anthony was in grade school, the two of us were curled up on the floor watching television after his homework was finished. I suddenly noticed the time.

"Oh no! You have to get to bed. It is school tomorrow."

He said, "I don't want to go to bed."

I said, "I don't blame you. Who wants to go to bed? Ugg! I hated going to bed when I was your age."

"So come on, get to bed."

He groaned, got up, and went to bed. He knew he had to get to bed. He just wanted me to share in his misery.

It is likely there has been little or no effective parenting in the homes of rebellious adolescents. One or both parents is/are missing, or is/are functionally missing. That is the parents are alcoholic, addicted to substances, or oblivious to the child's feelings and needs, &c.

There is, however, a line in dealing with rebellious teenagers. Some of them have been so wounded that the part of them that is human has been destroyed. These people are no longer able to imagine the feelings of another person. Life becomes a jungle—a series of destructive and illegal behavior that cannot be turned around.

At this point seeing, understanding, and psychological treatment becomes ineffective and futile.

The time to head off this kind of result is not in adolescence. Positive interactions must begin in childhood. In psychotherapy a patient has to feel 1) safe and 2) welcome in order for the work to progress successfully.

These same conditions must apply to effective parenting.

The vast number of scarred and ruined lives in adolescence bears glaring testimony to significant parenting failures. If a person has been raised and treated as an object, he or she will also treat others as objects—that is as entities without feelings. It is all he or she has known. It may seem illogical to do otherwise.

The most fortunate children have had an opportunity to be heard and have their feelings cared about by parents and others who have feelings and voices of their own. In a sense rebellion is simply an "end of the line" strategy to be heard and seen when all else has failed.

Seeing and hearing are essential. A person cannot find him or herself on his or her own. It is only in an *interaction* with a tuned in, empathic other that we are able to learn who we are. Children denied this experience are denied the identity structure upon which to build functioning adult lives (see also McWilliams, 1994).

Millions of people are not seen and are never found.

It is further the case that one cannot *sustain* oneself without being seen. One emerges to oneself in the exchanges of life across a wide range of contexts. It is the constant exchange with others—even if no or few words are spoken— that helps one correct erroneous ideas of him or herself. Without this one's sense of self gradually loses touch with the common experience of reality.

CHAPTER FOURTEEN: LEVELS OF SEEING

Not all seeing takes place at the same level. Some people can see more and farther than other people can.

Just as the view from the twentieth floor of a building is not the same as a view from the second floor, the view from different levels of seeing is not the same.

Levels concern the vertical dimension of seeing.

This is a phenomenon related to the issue of contexts. The smaller the context, the more limited the seeing will be. Conversely, the larger the context—or the more numerous the contexts experienced—the wider the seeing will be.

One who has never travelled beyond one's home town will not have the same breadth of seeing as one who has travelled to multiple foreign countries.

A person who is in elementary school will not have the same breadth of seeing and understanding as one who is in post graduate school.

Philip Larkin (1956/1989) wrote a poem that illustrates levels.

FIRST SIGHT

Lambs that learn to walk in snow
When their bleating clouds the air
Meet a vast unwelcome, know
Nothing but a sunless glare.
Newly stumbling to and fro
All they find outside the fold
Is a wretched width of cold.

As they wait beside the ewe,
Her fleeces wetly caked, there lies
Hidden round them, waiting too
Earth's immeasurable surprise.
They could not grasp it if they knew,
What so soon will wake and grow
Utterly unlike the snow.

The issue of levels is an important one when one is trying to see and understand another person. Typically, the more synoptic one's own level, the higher the probability is that he or she will be able to tune into another person.

As a general rule, problems tend to arise and exist on specific levels. *Sometimes* the problem can be solved by learning how to manage the elements on that level. This is usually how advice works.

Sometimes, however, the problem can only be solved by moving to a different level. This is where the situation gets complicated.

As I indicated in Chapter Seven, some people are open to new information and experience. Others wish to restrict their information and experience to where they are now.

People who are open to new experience tend to pursue learning and the experience of vastly new and different things. People who wish to restrict their experience tend to eschew these things.

If you wish to understand more than a few like minded and like experienced people, it is wise to be as open to new experience as possible.

There are certain specific experiences that tend to affect the level from which one is able to see.

One of these is a college education. There is something about obtaining a college education that separates one from those who have not gone to college. After such an experience one is able to see from a different perspective than one could before. Different things matter.

(College education here is used as involving the study of the *human experience*, not necessarily the STEM subjects [science, technology, engineering, mathematics]. These are more technical and do not directly center around human issues.)

Another factor that affects the level of experience is having a child. People who have a child find their perspective is different from what it was when they did not have a child. This difference can be profound. It is also difficult to have such an experience without actually having a child yourself.

Another factor is world travel. People who have been able to see their original context from the *outside* are able to have a different perspective from those who have only been able to see it from the *inside*. In addition to meeting people who are part of a context that looks at and lives life differently, one becomes powerfully aware of the different forms of experience life affords.

A further factor that changes the level from which one is able to see is the experience of profound love. Love can be transforming. It is wholly different from everyday life. There are levels of tenderness in love that exist nowhere else.

Those who are in love can attest to the difference in perspective that has entered their lives. This works for the huge experience of infatuation as well as for the quiet and disturbing depth of the discovery of abiding love. Both are life-changing.

And obviously related to this, another factor that changes levels of perception is the experience of catastrophe or profound tragedy. The baby dies. One's parents are killed in a car crash. One develops a terminal disease.

These experiences shift one's perspective in ways that are profound and transforming. We say, "The world is different now." We may begin to feel alienated from our former friends (who remain at another level).

Of course added to the above list should be the experience of significant psychotherapy or psychoanalysis. In such a process one is able to discover elements about oneself and others he or she could not see before. This profoundly changes one's perspective.

One becomes able to see more clearly and thus is able to have a more secure sense of who one really is as well as who others are. This allows one to fully be who one is and to be aware of being that person.

A colleague told me he routinely runs into young therapists who are highly religious. It is their view that they have the "right" view of things. For them, therapy consists in helping patients to get into compliance with these "right" views.

This is a disaster. It is also unethical.

Seeing and psychotherapy are harder than that. Such enterprises require one to see and understand where another person is before any consideration is made about what to do with that situation.

Further, the solution is best if it is found by the other person him or herself. A major part of the therapeutic work is constructing a foundation to allow for such a solution to be seen. That is, this new wider vision typically allows for more options to be considered.

At least it is hard to see how having more options is a bad thing.

The issue of levels is why there are times when the problem that is stated by a person is not the real problem. Often the issue is a problem precisely because it is only seen at the level it occurs.

There are therapy techniques that take the stated problem as the (entire) issue and work to solve that problem. These techniques may be good as far as they go. However, if one's experience is restricted to the one level where the problem occurred, it is entirely likely further problems will be encountered at that level that require solving.

This is to say that sometimes issues cannot be solved, because a solution to those issues does not exist at the level where the issue occurred. It is only by developing the ability to shift levels and therefore perspectives that the solution becomes readily apparent.

For example, I may feel others will admire me only if I appear to have no flaws. That's how it seems to me. I may not yet have learned it was only my father who responded to me when I appeared flawless. I haven't realized I am assuming people have the same view as my father.

Once I have learned this fact, I can see the world and other people differently. I don't need to be flawless to be admired. Imagine!

Sometimes a different level is made possible when I become aware of unconscious elements that are affecting *my own* way of seeing.

I had a patient who was very accomplished as an adult. He reported he suffered debilitating episodes of depression. This surprised me as he was so obviously capable — and he did not seem depressed in our sessions.

I commented that he did not seem outwardly depressed. He replied, "I get heard here."

We explored his background and discovered this man had experienced a terrifyingly violent mother. His father had been sidelined by her and was thus ineffectual as a protector of the patient.

The mother had routinely pointed out how deficient this boy was. He was severely criticized by her for the least of offenses. He could not remember her ever praising him. Though bright and likable among his school friends, he always felt something was wrong with him.

In fact, he still felt things were wrong with him at the time we met. When this material was discovered and made available to the patient, he found it hard to believe. His childhood treatment had been profound in shaping his outlook. Though he had lived through this childhood and attended a university in another state, he had always simply thought his mother's views were ordinary and correct— *even though* he recognized odd elements in them.

When his childhood pattern was discovered and explored, the patient was amazed he had never thought of this before—and his depression and difficulty with women was more understandable.

"I didn't have a chance," he told me tearfully.

What had happened was this person had experienced a shift in levels of seeing. In a sense he had developed the ability to see from a different point of view.

His brain had wired to the old training in the course of his development, and he would have to practice the new view over time in multiple situations in order to create new patterns of thinking and behaving as well as forming new neural pathways.

These new pathways would gradually become options to his original wiring. The view in terms of the new pathways would be dramatically different from the view from the old pathways.

Foucault (1994) realized that the context (i.e., point of view) influenced what is seen. What is seen *along with* the point of view is important. That is, what is seen owes much to the place from which the seeing was done. People don't see the same things, because they don't stand in the same place. They don't have the same thoughts and feelings.

Levels of seeing are always important. They influence the world we are able to find.

CHAPTER FIFTEEN: ISSUES OF ATTACHMENT

The area of attachment concerns the bond that is established between a child and his or her mother at the beginning of life.

An optimal relationship is one in which the child is made to feel 1) safe and 2) welcome.

In such an environment the child is able to learn he or she is wanted and thus is desirable as a person. He or she is able to learn to explore the world around him or her—and that failure is simply part of the deal.

More importantly the child's first "other" is experienced as trustworthy and welcoming. This will be where the child will start his or her journey toward learning about all the other people in the world.

The closer such an optimal representation is approximated, the more the child will develop what is called *secure* attachment.

This is a situation in which the child is able to internalize a safe and welcoming other. The child is also able to internalize a positive view of him or herself. These elements, being now internalized, will be present for the child even when he or she is not interacting with another.

Also when people are like the mother, they are assumed to be safe and welcoming. Such a child is less fearful of the world. Also the child is drawn to healthier people who are able to create and maintain resonant interactions.

Obviously several things can go wrong with the beginning mother-child interaction.

One of these is when the mother fails to establish a safe and welcoming space. Like the woman (with the phone) in the coffee shop, she may be preoccupied with other things. She may not truly want this child and to her the child may be a burden.

Such a child will likely develop a *detached* form of attachment. He or she will feel it is pointless to reach out to others. Others are seen as only interested in themselves. If such a child has a need, he or she must solve it him or herself—others will not care or help.

A detached child will have difficulties in interpersonal interactions and will have difficulty establishing intimate relationships—or even seeing the virtue of such things.

Chronically lonely, such a person will essentially live a life of interpersonal indifference. Relationships will not be valued.

Another situation is one in which the mother is able to be safe and welcoming *some* of the time. In such a situation the child will not know what to expect on any given instance. This leads to an attachment pattern known as *ambivalent*.

Ambivalent children are, in a sense, caught between approaching mother and others on the one hand and avoiding them on the other.   They move back and forth between these poles and are never able to be sure whether the relationships they have are secure or not.

This quality of never being sure tends to permeate all interactions they have with others.   They can never be sure of anything when it comes to relationships.   They never are able to know "where they stand."

A fourth kind of attachment pattern is called *chaotic*. This is a situation in which the child's background was itself chaotic.   That is the early environment was all over the place and made no reliable sense.   In such a situation there was no *consistency*.

For such a child the world remains all over the place. There is nothing that can truly be trusted or relied upon for long.   Events tend to be either good or bad, and these qualities are constantly in flux.   Life is crazy-making.

This is the case as good and bad are basic categories and, as such, do not fit very many people or situations exactly. Rather, we *tend* to move closer or farther away from one or another of them.

Why is this important?

The attachment pattern of a person conveys a great deal of information about him or her.   It tells you, for example, what his or her relationship behavior is likely to be.   It also tells you what importance relationship interactions will be to him or her.

Attachment patterns may not be apparent on a first meeting. It is only by interacting with a person over a period of time that they may become apparent.

One of the reasons to become involved in significant psychotherapy is that such an enterprise allows for an opportunity to *redo* the attachment experience. That is, one has an opportunity to attach to a new person—the therapist. Further, a competent psychotherapist will be able to create an environment that promotes secure attachment.

Here the therapist is able to function as a secure mother and create a situation in which the patient feels safe and welcome. Also the patient will be able to experience empathic emotional resonance—possibly for the first time.

As the treatment is extended, the new context of therapy may be tested, experienced and internalized in itself. Therapy becomes a different kind of "world" in which new ideas, feelings, and behaviors can be tried out.

In this environment, the present treatment can be contrasted with one's own early history, and the differences can be seen and understood. Also the wiring to the therapeutic environment will be different from the original wiring to the childhood context. The old attachment experience and wiring will remain primary, but the new attachment experience and wiring will be secondary.

This is the magic.

The goal of such treatment is to provide one with an ability to 1) see these differences between new and old patterns and 2) to *choose* between them. It is this ability to choose that frees one from an obligatory dependency on the old pattern.

It is a difference between new life and old life.

As mentioned earlier the new life experience allows one to have a different point of view than he or she had before. One's own history can be seen differently from this new point of view. Some problems that could not be solved before will be solvable in light of the new ability.

Additionally, routine relationship conflicts are often able to be seen and understood when the attachment patterns involved are discovered and illuminated. Suddenly the conflict makes sense.

In order for this effect to be possible the therapist must be capable of *finding* the patient. The empathic resonance required to create optimal attachment experiences requires such a level of seeing and feeling. That is the patient is seen, heard, and *felt*.

It must be pointed out that, obviously, everyone in the world is not safe and welcoming, and therefore a distrusting attitude can be beneficial. While this is clearly the case, the issue raised here concerns intimacy and psychotherapy.

It is one thing to be *capable* of feeling safe and welcome and quite another to never or almost never experience these things. Being capable is not the same thing as being forced. Attaining the capacity to successfully engage in intimacy and significant psychotherapy simply adds capability to other kinds of interaction patterns.

A sad truth is that people tend to attract like others in attachment styles. Thus secure people tend to find other secure people, &c. And while it is true not all therapists have been able to develop secure attachment abilities, some of them have. Those are the therapists that can be of most help to one with problems in this area.

CHAPTER SIXTEEN: SEEING IN HINDSIGHT

Sometimes factors cannot be seen in the middle of an interaction. It is only in reflection that such things appear and command attention.

This is true as the interaction itself may be filled with many factors that may or may not help in the development of an adequate perception of the situation.

For one thing momentary emotional effects can cloud a clear picture. Also details of a description may catch one's attention and other elements are missed.

This will be especially true if the person to whom one is speaking is being manipulative, overly vague, threatening or any number of emotionally compelling situations.

When the pressure on one is so intense one feels one cannot be who he or she is, or cannot respond in an open and honest way, it is important to notice this as it comprises important information in coming to an understanding of the other.

Why does he or she need to come on so strong? What is this about?

If you feel you cannot be seen or heard for who you are, this is telling you the other person needs "reality" to be a certain way. He or she is unable to simply deal with things the way they are. A free-flowing dialog may be impossible.

In such situations it is also important to realize there is important information that is being excluded. In psychotherapy it would be important at some point to attempt to discover what this is and why it must be excluded.

Away from the situation it will be easier to see that this interaction pattern has been in use. One will likely be at calm and able to respond in more familiar ways.

When one thinks about an interaction in retrospect, the live elements in the interaction are missing. One only has an overall sense upon which to focus.

This is why it is routinely important to *listen again*. Often one must listen again and again and again before elements are heard or understood at any level of depth.

Also it is helpful to *revisit* interactions and/or information in searching for a new perspective or viewpoint.

Patients often wonder if I am tired of hearing "the same old story." The answer is "no." Information and insights may be picked up in a subsequent retelling that I missed earlier.

It is not uncommon that insights will occur to one while talking to other people, experiencing other situations, or even when staring at the wall.

Related to these issues is the very helpful exercise of trying to *disconfirm* one's own views and theories in general—and especially about another person.

That is, it is important to ask how is my seeing and understanding of this other person slanted or simply wrong?

The search for disconfirming evidence is part of the bedrock foundation of science, and for good reason.

It is possible for us to become stuck in a point of view and thus unable to see other points of view as being credible. The term for this is *aspect blindness*. I can see certain aspects of something or someone but not others.

For example, "I can see Rome as *different* but not as *stunning.*"

Why not? Why not try to put yourself in place to have a different view from the one you have now?

I might, for example, ask others who know some person what their views on him or her are. Others will likely have a different perspective or may be able to add some facet I have not yet considered.

I might even ask the person him or herself, "What don't I see?" This is actually a very good question to ask a child.

On the other hand, asking your girlfriends or boyfriends what they think of someone *may* not be the wisest thing to do. The reason for this is that people often respond in ways they feel you want them to respond—or they respond in ways they know will be socially acceptable.

In hindsight one may discover another person seems to be hiding behind a *facade*.

We as people use masks for all kinds of reasons, but by and large, when we use a mask we are using it on purpose. That is, it is a solution to some sort of problem.

When I pretend to be something or someone I do not feel I am, I create a false interaction field. It is not the case I am always able to fool others wholesale. Others often receive a *mixed message*. My emotional communication may differ from my verbal communication. This says I am pretending something.

Others will be fooled only if they want to be fooled or when they agree to go along with the distortion.

Needless to say pretending does not further either intimacy or psychotherapy. It may, however, cover a weakness or wound that needs protection from ordinary discourse.

Often it is discovered in hindsight that one has a need or impulse to forgive one's parents and those who were not available in one's background.

One's parents were limited. It is true. They were flawed, human creatures. They too had limited parents. This is how they became limited. One's parents wounded one. It is likely they were wounded in similar fashion—and perhaps much worse.

It is entirely appropriate to be angry at one's parents for how they hurt or neglected one. That is what they did.

The wound, however, is *mine*. *I* am the one they wounded. Since the wound is mine, it is *my* issue to deal with; not theirs. If I don't deal with it, I am the one who will be compromised, not them.

Reality is always busily being what it is. The only way we can be part of it is to be limited ourselves and have limited parents and limited friends and lovers.

We also produce limited children.

None of this *needs* to be an overwhelming problem. It is simply the way reality works. The thing to do when one realizes one's limits, is to seek help in dealing with them. Both ourselves and everyone around us will benefit from that effort.

CHAPTER SEVENTEEN: SUMMARY

The issue discussed here has been the seeing and understanding of another person in a way that allows for intimacy and/or psychotherapy.

The question is how do you see a person *on the inside*?

Intimacy and psychotherapy have been found to be "intimately" related to each other. Psychotherapy is a subset of intimacy in which any romantic feelings, if any, are not acted upon. Psychotherapy is a place where only talk is allowed, but it is also a place where every form of talk is allowed and even encouraged.

The instructions for psychoanalysis are 1) say whatever comes to your mind and 2) say everything that comes to your mind.

There are enormous benefits that come from such a system. The therapist is not a judge. He or she cannot tell one what he or she should do. Nor can he or she decide whether or not one is a worth-while person. He or she simply assumes one is.

I can talk to the therapist about things I would never tell anyone else for the simple reason the therapist won't betray me by telling others what I have said.   Whatever it is, it stays between us.

(This is the case unless I have broken a major law and a judge *orders* my therapist to reveal information.   Still in some states, even then, my therapist may not disclose this material.)

The therapist does not have to live in my life—at least more than in a restricted way.   He or she is thus able to have a different perspective of me than I can have.   As he or she learns more about me, both an inside and an outside view become possible.

We live in a culture that doesn't necessarily value intimacy and personal psychological development.   We value achievement and the ability to generate wealth.   If those things are not within reach of my own group, attitudes and belonging to certain groups may take their place.

Let's face it, a culture that is primarily focused on efficiency often loses touch with people in their human or complete sense.

We have not come from perfect homes.   It could be that we have never before experienced an interaction with a warm, accepting and affirming other—let alone a working intimacy.   Our backgrounds may, and often have, included the experience of trauma and profound negative occurrences.

We have likely been scarred in love and have experienced profoundly hurtful events related to relationships.

The amount of negative and difficult things that could happen to us are legion.

It is not uncommon for us to need some significant period of healing before we are able to strike out again into our own deeper areas. This is where we run into another value in our culture: *self-reliance.*

We are supposed to be strong and capable. We are not supposed to show weakness. We are supposed to keep a "strong upper lip." Showing weakness immediately identifies us as wanting or as being less than others.

In fact, we are even reluctant to discuss health sorts of problems we may have *with our own physicians.* We minimize problems and only seek the assistance of physicians when the problem has reached significant proportions— when it is difficult, if even possible, to cure.

And forget about therapists! Get serious. They only exist for *crazy people.* You know, *weirdos.* Also we were taught by our parents we should manage our issues ourselves. Like our parents did. And not seek treatment.

This kind of approach didn't work for our parents, and it will not work for us. As we would have loved for our parents to seek psychological assistance, so our children wish we would.

These comments are especially true if we or our parents are of the strict variety. We are supposed to know everything and be all capable. That, the story goes, is the only way to be on top. And, of course, that is where we want to be. Others are inferior.

Let's face it. Putting oneself in a position to learn more is *not* a weakness. It is a strength. Those who learn more are of invaluable worth to the world and to our lives.

It is a similar situation with reference to learning more about our psychological issues. The more we are able to discover and learn, the more of a resource we will be not only to ourselves but to the people around us.

Every street that has a reasonably mentally healthy person living on it is a better place to live.

To improve our abilities at intimacy and at psychotherapy it is important to learn to see better. An adequate understanding of ourselves or others requires us to see as much as possible—and to see as finely as possible. This allows subtlety and nuance to become part of the equation.

When I was in Phnom Penh visiting my son who was there with others from his law school class, I visited the Royal Palace. It was very hot, and I was becoming dehydrated. I decided to set off for an area of the city where I knew there were several restaurants, and I could get something to drink.

Between where I was and these restaurants was an area of town I had been warned to avoid. Foreigners were always coming to grief there. Avoiding this section, however, would have required me to go a considerable distance out of the way.

"To hell with it," I thought and plowed straight ahead.

The "forbidden" sector consisted of a dirt road that was flanked on both sides by crude shacks. As I walked down the middle of that road, I noticed a little girl—perhaps three years old—who was playing in the middle of the road. She was very dirty, and her dress was torn.

As I approached her she eyed me apprehensively. I smiled and said, "Hi." She sheepishly returned my smile. Then I continued along the road. At once I became aware of a tapping on my leg. I turned around, and this little girl handed me a small rock. We both smiled, and I said "Thank you."

She had given me what she had, because I had been kind to her and had taken the time to acknowledge her, a person of worth. She was really very beautiful.

It wasn't until later it occurred to me no one would have done that on the street where I live in the United States. We just don't do things like that.

I still have the rock.

NOTE ON SEEING

The ability to see reality as it is, largely unhampered by distortions, defenses, and untoward motivations hinges on a general lack of trauma in one's process of learning to see. There are many things it is difficult for us to see, and we need support and care in developing the ability to perform this function. At first, the child must be helped to come to grips with the fact he or she is dependent on others, outside the self, for survival. This occurs when the child discovers he or she is dependent on the mother's breast for nourishment. Learning about this dependency involves a primitive sort of humiliation, as the child must learn he or she is not entirely in control of his or her world. That is the child is not self-sufficient. With this realization the child feels weak and vulnerable and must be helped to learn worth and capacity.

The child must also be helped to navigate the realization that the mother loves more people than the infant. She has other things to do. Since mother is the source of goodness to the infant, it is threatening to have this goodness involved elsewhere. The child must be helped to learn that, even with mother's other points of interest, there is still enough (genuine) love for him or her (see Steiner, 1993, 2006, and Money-Kyrle, 1968, 1978).

It is at this point that catastrophic failure creates life-long damage. For the child to lose goodness in life leads to the notion reality is dangerous or bad. What is the point of struggling with reality if there is no goodness to be had? Such a child is likely to develop a narcissistic orientation and to hold that goodness is within him or herself. This creates a gap with reality and a withdrawal to the ego-centric position. The affairs of the self will be preferred over reality.

In order to manage intense feelings of badness associated with the loss of the good (i.e. not being worthy of the good), the child will become a candidate for grandiosity and elevated self-regard. With the necessity to maintain this inflated view of the self or else risk re-experiencing worthlessness, the child's energy will be siphoned away from learning more about reality, other people, the self, and the world. Further, the maintenance of such an adjustment impairs the ability to see and be seen. Being (genuinely) seen becomes a threat to the artificial grandiose image that covers shame. Also being able to see the world accurately threatens the maintenance of this grandiose image as it reveals that others see one as an inflated construction instead of a true human person.

Ultimately the child will be required to face the fact of death. How well this is accomplished has significant consequences for both seeing and being seen. The denial of death along with the assumption that life continues forever creates a world view that distorts a constituting fact of life. The terrible brevity of life must be seen as a factor in the reverence accorded to the preciousness of other lives, opportunities, and, ultimately, existence itself. It is a task of healthy psychological functioning to grieve one's youthful arrogance and excess. These things must be slowly replaced by an awareness of one's own small stature in a cosmos in which all things come to an end. This is not so much a tragedy as it is the nature of things. Goodness is sacred.

In a way the self develops through losses. People once grandly thought the Earth was the center of the solar system. All things revolved around us. To move beyond this view required the development of better ways of seeing. The child of each of us must learn to see the people of the world as well as ourselves in terms of our humanness, the difficulties we have, and our separate existence. This allows us to put ourselves in each other's place to a significant degree. It is in this sense we can be said to be one family.

Psychotherapy is an experience in which seeing plays an essential part. Success depends upon how much the therapist is able to see and understand. It is important for us as patients to learn to allow ourselves to be seen—really seen, nothing held back. We as patients, also, must be able to see the therapist well enough to feel we can trust that he or she has the empathic capacity to genuinely see us as well as the capacity to help us become more genuine and more available to reality. It is this process that allows us to progress beyond the limitations of our backgrounds and development.

It is in this sense imagination becomes such an asset. Developed capacity for imagination requires a firm floor (reality) upon which to stand. This allows one to "disappear" into fantasy without losing the way back. Greater flights of fantasy and creativity are possible for those who have a firm notion of reality (see Freud, 1908).

The same can be said of love. Entering the world of love involves entering a special place with another. To be able to do this, one must be able to extend beyond oneself to become connected to another and *at the same time* be able to find one's way back to oneself. This is what creates the emotional bond. Another can be in my world and still be another. That is the walls of the self become permeable and allow empathic interaction with another. It is this respectful and warm consideration of another as being worthy of the same care and regard one accords oneself that creates the emotional power of such an experience.

Love also inevitably requires us to develop an ability to see the hurt and sacrifice we have required of the loved one. It is this expanded complex of awareness that allows love to deepen beyond excitement and pleasure in order zto become transforming and profound.

REFERENCES

Ambrose, A. Wittgenstein's Lectures: Cambridge 1932-1935. Roman and Littlefield. 1979.

Andersen, H. C. The Little Match Girl. Puffin. 2001.

Aristotle. History of Animals (*Historia Animalium*) See: http://www.ucmp.berkeley.edu/history/aristotle.html

http://davesgarden.com/guides/articles/view/2051/#b

Bartholomew, K. Avoidance of Intimacy: An Attachment Perspective. Journal of Social and Personal Relationships May, 1990, vol. 7(2) 147-178.

Beier, E.G. The Silent Language of Psychotherapy. Aldine, 1966.

Benjamin, J. The Bonds of Love, Pantheon, 1988.

Benjamin, J. Like Subjects, Love Objects: Essays on Recognition and Sexual Difference. Yale, 1995.

Bowlby, J. A Secure Base: Clinical Applications of Attachment Theory. Hogarth, 1969/1980.

Bowlby, J. A Secure Base: Parent-Child Attachment and Healthy Human Development. Basic, 1988.

Campbell, J. The Hero With a Thousand Faces. Princeton/ Bollingen. 1949/1973.

Campbell, J. Transformations of Myth Through Time. Harper, 1990.

Campbell, J. The Inner Reaches of Outer Space: Metaphor as Myth and Religion. A. van der Marck, 1985.

Camus, A. The Fall. Vintage. 1956.

Cavell, S. Must We Mean What We Say? Cambridge, 1969/2002.

Cooper, J. and Maxwell, N. (Eds.) Narcissistic Wounds. Aronson, 1995.

Crane, H. The Complete Poems of Hart Crane. Double-day. 1958.

Derrida, J. and Kamuf, P. A Derrida Reader: Between the Blinds. Columbia. 1991.

Derrida, J. and Spivak, G.C. Of Grammatology. Johns Hopkins. 2016.

Eliade, M. Myth and Reality, Harper, 1963.

Eliade, M. The Sacred and the Profane, Harcourt, 1957.

Firestone, R. W. and Catlett, J. Fear of Intimacy. APA, 1999.

Flax, J. Thinking Fragments: Psychoanalysis, Feminism, and Postmodernism in the Contemporary West. California, 1990.

Foucault, M. The Order of Things: An Archeology of the Human Sciences. Vintage. 1970/1994.

Freud, S. 1908. "Creative Writers and Day-Dreaming." *SE* 9: pp. 141–154.

Gabbard, G. O. Psychodynamic Psychiatry in Clinical Practice. American Psychiatric Press. 2000.

Gabbard, G. O. Long-Term Psychodynamic Psychotherapy. American Psychiatric Press. 2004.

Gadamer, H-G. Truth and Method (Bloomsbury Revelations). Bloomsbury Academic. 2013.

Gadamer, H-G. and Linge, D.E. Philosophical Hermeneutics. California. 2008.

Gill, J.D. Forms of Life and Other Essays. Create Space. 2014.

Gill, J.D. Finding Human. Create Space. 2014.

Gill, J.D. The Misery of the Good Child. Create Space. 2015.

Giovacchini, P. L. A Narrative Textbook of Psychoanalysis. Aronson, 1987.

Hatfield, E. and Rapson, R. L. Love, Sex, and Intimacy: Their psychology, Biology, and History. HarperCollins. 1993.

Irigaray, L. Speculum of the Other Woman. Cornell. 1974/1985.

Irigaray, L. This Sex Which Is Not One. Cornell. 1977/1985.

Kohut, H. How Does Analysis Cure? Chicago, 1984.

Kohut, H. http://www.sfu.ca/~psimpson/ kohutppr1.htm#to)

Lakoff, G. Understanding Trump. https://georgelakoff.com/ 2016/07/23/understanding-trump-2/

Larkin, P. Collected Poems. F.S.G. 1989.

Laurenceau, J.-P., Barrett, L. F., and Pietromonaco, P. R. Intimacy as an interpersonal process: The importance of self-disclosure, partner disclosure, and perceived partner responsiveness in interpersonal exchanges. Journal of Personality and Social Psychology, Vol 74(5), May 1998, 1238-1251.

McWilliams, N. Psychoanalytic Diagnosis: Understanding Personality Structures in the Clinical Process. Guilford, 1994.

McWilliams, N. Psychoanalytic Case Formulation. Guilford, 1999.

Mollen, P. The Fragile Self. Aronson, 1993.

Money-Kyrle, R. "Cognitive Development." International Journal of Psycho-Analysis, 1968, 49, pp. 691–698. Reprinted in The Collected Papers of Roger Money-Kyrle, Clunie Press, 1978, pp. 416–433

Money-Kyrle, R. "The aim of Psycho-Analysis." International Journal of Psycho-Analysis, 1971, 52, pp. 103–106. Reprinted in The Collected Papers of Roger Money-Kyrle, Clunie Press ,1978, pp. 442-449.

O'Connor, F. Wise Blood. FSG. 1949/1962/1990.

Ogden, T.H. The Analytic Third: An Overview. http://www. psychematters.com/papers/ogden.htm 2001.

Page, K.J. The Psychology of Intimacy. Guilford. 1997.

Rosenthal, R. https://sites.google.com/site/7arosenthal/

Rosenthal, R., and Rosnow, R.L. Artifacts in Behavioral Research. Oxford. 2009.

Saint-Exupery, A. Le Petit Prince. Gallimard, 1940.

Saint-Exupery, A. The Little Prince. Harcourt. 1943.

Shakespeare, W. Macbeth. In: Harrison, G. B. Major Plays and the Sonnetts. Harcourt. 1948. p. 841.

Sparrow, S. Religious Vision and Free Will in Flannery O'Connor's Novel Wise Blood. http://www.catholiceducation.org/en/culture/art/religious-vision-and-free-will-in-flannery-o-connor-s-novel-wise-blood.html

Steiner, J. Psychic Retreats: Pathological Organisations of the Personality in Psychotic, Neurotic, and Borderline Patients. Routledge, 1993.

Steiner, J. "Seeing and Being Seen: Narcissistic Pride and Narcissistic Humiliation." The International Journal of Psychoanalysis, 2006, 87, pp. 939–951.

Sutter, R. Interpreting Wittgenstein: A Cloud of Philosophy, A Drop of Grammar. Temple. 1989.

Tatkin, S., and Hendrix, H. Wired for Love: How Understanding Your Partner's Brain and Attachment Style Can Help You Defuse Conflict and Build a Secure Relationship. New Harbinger. 2012.

Wittgenstein, L. Philosophical Investigations. Macmillan, 1953.

Wittgenstein, L. The Blue and Brown Books. Harper. 1958/1965.

Zimmer, H. The King and the Corpse. Princeton/Bollingen. 1948/1993.

ABOUT THE AUTHOR

J.D. Gill is a clinical psychologist at the University of Utah. She is an Adjunct Associate Professor of Psychology, a Clinical Professor of Counseling Psychology, and an Adjunct Associate Professor of Psychiatry in the University of Utah School of Medicine. Dr. Gill maintains a busy practice at the University of Utah.

Dr. Gill has degrees in English Literature, Philosophy, Psychology, and two post docs in psychoanalytic psychotherapy. She studied in the Writing Program at the University of Utah. She has been a practicing psychologist for over forty years and has presented over five hundred seminars, lectures, workshops, and papers. A world traveler, Dr. Gill has actively sought to experience multiple viewpoints and perspectives.

www.ingramcontent.com/pod-product-compliance
Lightning Source LLC
Chambersburg PA
CBHW070115290526
45789CB00005B/2029